The Time of the LORD's Favor Has Come

Terri Tidwell

Copyright © 2024 Terri Tidwell

All rights reserved.

ISBN:

DEDICATION

I want to dedicate this book to God, my Father, the God of all creation, the One who said, "Let there be light," and there was light. (Genesis 1:3).

I want to dedicate this book to Jesus, the Son of the Living God, the Word that gave life to everything that was created, and His life brought light to everyone. This light shines in the darkness, and the darkness can never extinguish it. (John 1:4-5).

I want to dedicate this book to the Spirit of God. The Spirit alone gives eternal life. Human effort accomplishes nothing. And the very Words I have spoken to you are Spirit and Life. (John 6:63).

CONTENTS

	Acknowledgments	i
1	Introduction	Pg 3
2	What Does God's Favor Look Like?	Pg 7
3	What Does God's Love Look Like?	Pg 9
4	The New Way	Pg 13
5	The High Cost of Following Jesus	Pg 18
6	How Does God Love His People?	Pg 26
7	What Does Divine Discipline Look Like?	Pg 33
8	Blessings and Curses Both Come from God	Pg 42
9	How to Find God's Favor in our Finances	Pg 50
10	How to Find God's Favor in our Relationships	Pg 62
11	God is Looking for Certain Responses in His Children	Pg 82
12	Open Your Mouth Wide and I will Fill it With Good Things	Pg 96
13	Be Ready to Suffer	Pg 100
14	God will Make Us an Immovable Rock	Pg 105
15	God will Pour Out a Spirit of Grace and Prayer	Pg 110
16	Conclusion	Pg 122

ACKNOWLEDGMENTS

I want to thank my husband, Lyndyl Tidwell, who is my best friend. He, too, has opened his heart wide to receive the truths found in this book.

Before He went to the cross, Jesus said, "I pray that they will all be one, just as you and I are one – as You are in Me, Father, and I am in You. And may they be in us so that the world will believe You sent Me. I have given them the glory You gave Me, so they may be one as we are one. I am in them and You are in Me. May they experience such perfect unity that the world will know that You sent Me and that You love them as much as You love Me." (John 17:21-23).

Through the daily Bible readings and prayer and the writing of this book, my husband and I are experiencing a unity that we have never experienced before. It is glorious. May you, too, experience this unity of the spirit as you join our journey in coming to know God in ways we have never known Him. May we all come to know how high and wide and long and deep His love is and may we all experience that love that is past understanding.

1 INTRODUCTION

The time of the LORD's favor has come!

In December of 2023, the LORD gave me a Word. "The end of the world is coming soon. Therefore, be earnest and disciplined in your prayers." (1 Peter 4:7).

I took this Word very seriously – it is time to pray! Then a thought entered my mind that I would like to record all the Words that the LORD had given me over the years, so I started to blog. What I wrote was much too long for a blog, so I wrote a book instead: THE PROPHETS SPEAK. In that book, I wrote down everything the LORD had been speaking to me over my lifetime. I left nothing out. When I got through, I was in shock. It was all right there in black and white – unabridged, unadulterated. God's plan.

The LORD gave this message to Zephaniah. "I will sweep away everything from the face of the earth," says the LORD. "I will sweep away people and animals alike. I will sweep away the birds of the sky and the fish in the sea. I will reduce the wicked to heaps of rubble, and I will wipe humanity from the face of the earth," says the LORD. Your silver and gold will not save you on that Day of the LORD's anger. For the whole land will be devoured by the fire of His jealousy. He will make a terrifying end of all the people on earth. (Zephaniah 1:2-3, 18). Then Ezekiel 21 tells us God is about to unsheathe His sword, and when He does, both the righteous and the unrighteous alike will perish. There will be a Day when God will make a terrifying end of all the people on the earth.

My jaw dropped when I saw it all written together. Everyone is going to die. I wanted to apologize for this Word, but the LORD said, "Don't apologize. This is My plan, a plan to prosper and not to harm, a plan to give hope and a future." And the LORD said, "But for those who are righteous, the way is not steep and rough. You are a God who does what is right, and You smooth out the path ahead of them. LORD, we show our trust in you by obeying your laws; our heart's desire is to glorify your name. In the night I search for You; in the morning I earnestly seek You. For only when You come to judge the earth will people learn what is right." (Isaiah 26:7-9). It is only when God comes to judge the earth that we will we learn what is right.

Then the day I pushed "send" to publish that book, January 16, 2024, the LORD gave me this scripture:

Again, a message came to me from the LORD: "Son of man, you've heard that proverb they quote in Israel: 'Time passes, and prophecies come to nothing.' Tell the people, 'This is what the Sovereign LORD says: I will put an end to this proverb, and you will soon stop quoting it.' Now give them this new proverb to replace the old one: 'The time has come for every prophecy to be fulfilled!'

"There will be no more false visions and flattering predictions in Israel. For I am the LORD! If I say it, it will happen. There will be no more delays, you rebels of Israel. I will fulfill My threat of destruction in your own lifetime. I, the Sovereign LORD, have spoken!" (Ezekiel 12:21-28).

When I saw this message, I took it seriously. All these things will happen in our lifetime. There will be no more delay. The LORD is about to pour out His fury on the whole earth.

But then the next day, January 17, 2024, the LORD started speaking a new Word over me: "The time of the LORD's favor has come." What??? It is true! In the middle of this time of judgment, the LORD is going to do kind, kind things for His people. We will all experience the LORD'S favor. For several months now, I have been meditating on what that means. I don't want to speculate. I want to give a clear message.

"But now, O Jacob, listen to the LORD who created you. O Israel, the One who formed you says, 'Do not be afraid, for I have ransomed you. I have called you by name; you are mine. When you go through deep waters, I will be with you. When you go through rivers of difficulty, you will not drown. When you walk through the fire of oppression, you will not be burned up; the flames will not consume you. For I am the LORD, your God, the Holy One of Israel, your Savior. I gave Egypt as a ransom for your freedom; I gave Ethiopia and Seba in your place. Others were given in exchange for you. I traded their lives for yours because you are precious to Me. You are honored, and I love you.'"

"Do not be afraid, for I am with you. I will gather you and your children from east and west. I will say to the north and south, 'Bring My sons and daughters back to Israel from the distant corners of the earth. Bring all who claim Me as their God, for I have made them for My glory. It was I who created them.'"

"Bring out the people who have eyes but are blind, who have ears but are deaf. Gather the nations together! Assemble the peoples of the world! Which of their idols has ever foretold such things? Which can predict what will happen tomorrow? Where are the witnesses of such predictions? Who can verify that they spoke the truth?"

"But you are My witnesses, O Israel!" says the LORD. "You are My servant. You have been chosen to know Me, believe in Me, and understand that I alone am God. There is no other God – there never has been, and there never will be. I, yes I, am the LORD, and there is no other Savior. First, I predicted your rescue, then I saved you and proclaimed it to the world. No foreign god has ever done this. You are witnesses that I am the only God," says the LORD. "From eternity to eternity I am God. No one can snatch anyone out of My hand. No one can undo what I have done." (Isaiah 43:1-13).

God is telling us all what He is going to do in advance. He tells us that He is going to rescue us, and then we will watch Him do it. We will see all these things happen. We will experience His goodness. We have been chosen to know Him, to believe in Him, and to understand that He alone is God. We have been chosen to be His witnesses! We will all see and declare that there is a God in heaven who does whatever He pleases. He is a good God, and He has a good plan, a plan to prosper and not to harm, a plan to give hope and a future. In the middle of His wrath, God is sending favor. Wow! I was halfway through writing this book when God revealed to me what that favor looked like. I had no idea. So, I started over.

2 WHAT DOES GOD'S FAVOR LOOK LIKE?

When I started writing this book, I didn't want to speculate what the favor of God would look like. I want to send a clear message, a clear trumpet call. I started writing, and while I was writing, the LORD opened my eyes to see things I had never seen before. I am trembling with excitement at what I saw.

"Since you have heard about Jesus and have learned the truth that comes from Him, throw off your old sinful nature and your former way of life, which is corrupted by lust and deception. Instead, let the Spirit renew your thoughts and attitudes. Put on your new nature, created to be like God – truly righteous and holy." (Ephesians 4:21-24). What? We are created to be like God? LIKE GOD? So, I asked God, what are You like? And He took me to 1 John.

"We know how much God loves us, and we put our trust in His love. God is love, and all who live in love live in God, and God lives in them. And as we live in God, our love grows more perfect. So we will not be afraid on the Day of judgment, but we can face Him with confidence because we live like Jesus here in this world. Such love has no fear, because perfect love expels all fear. If we are afraid, it is for fear of punishment, and this shows that we have not fully experienced His perfect love. We love each other because He loved us first." (1 John 4:16-19).

PERFECT LOVE. Wow! God's favor is that we will all walk in perfect love. We will all live like Jesus here in this world. Even in this Day of wrath when things get cruel and crazy, God's people will live in love. This perfect love will cast out all fear, because fear is for fear of punishment. Perfect love casts out fear.

When I saw this, the skies opened above me, and every Word that God had ever spoken to me came alive. LOVE. It is all about love. In the coming days, we, God's people, will let the Spirit change our thoughts and attitudes. We will take off our old sinful nature, which is corrupted by lust and deception, and we will put on our new nature – love. Then we will become LIKE GOD – truly righteous and holy. LOVE. It is all about love. God's favor is that we will live in love. And the time of the LORD's favor has come. This is bigger than I could have ever imagined.

3 WHAT DOES GOD'S LOVE LOOK LIKE?

When we think of love, we think of something that is going to make us feel good, but God's love is not about what we get, it is about what we give. A lot of times when we love others, we get nothing in return, or worse than that, we get hatred and hostility. So, we will not be doing ourselves a favor if we think that loving others will be easy or that it will feel good. It will not. It will be an act of obedience, and most of the time it will come with a great cost.

"You have heard the law that says the punishment must match the injury: 'An eye for an eye, and a tooth for a tooth.' But I say, do not resist an evil person!" What??? "If someone slaps you on the right cheek, offer the other cheek also. If you are sued in court and your shirt is taken from you, give your coat, too. If a soldier demands that you carry his gear for a mile, carry it two miles. Give to those who ask, and don't turn away from those who want to borrow." (Matthew 5:38-42).

Don't resist an evil person? If someone wants to hurt us, let him? If someone wants to take from us, let him? If someone demands that we do something, we do it? Not only do we let him hurt us, take from us, and make demands, but we give him more??? We give to those who ask, and we don't turn away from those who want to borrow?

There is no way in our own selves that we could do what God is asking His people to do here, our selfish nature would not let us. That is why we must let the Spirit change our thoughts and attitudes. We must put on our new nature and learn to know our Creator and become like Him, truly righteous and holy. We must keep turning to Jesus so that He can remove the veil and we can find freedom. Then we can see and reflect

His glory. Then we can love like He loves.

"You have heard the law that says, 'Love your neighbor' and hate your enemy. But I say, love your enemies! Pray for those who persecute you! In that way, you will be acting as true children of your Father in heaven. For He gives His sunlight to both the evil and the good, and He sends rain on the just and the unjust alike. If you love only those who love you, what reward is there for that? Even corrupt tax collectors do that much. If you are kind only to your friends, how are you different from anyone else? Even pagans do that. But you are to be perfect, even as your Father in heaven is perfect." (Matthew 5:43-48).

Perfect. Perfect love. God wants His children to be perfect because He is perfect. If we can learn to do this while we are on this earth, we will be like God. WE WILL BE LIKE GOD! "God is love, and all who live in love live in God, and God lives in them. And as we live in God, our love grows more perfect. So we will not be afraid on the Day of judgment, but we can face Him with confidence because we live like Jesus here in this world." (1 John 4:16-17).

I have never in my lifetime met anyone who loves like this. I do not love like this. But in the coming days, there will be a lot of perfect people in this world. We will see more and more of the goodness of God in the land of the living.

"And so, dear brothers and sisters, I plead with you to give your bodies to God because of all He has done for you. Let them be a living and holy sacrifice – the kind He will find acceptable. This is the way to worship Him. Don't copy the behavior and customs of this world, but let God transform you into a new person by changing the way you think. Then you will learn to know God's will for you, which is good and pleasing and perfect."

"Because of the privilege and authority God has given me, I give each of you this warning: Don't think you are better than you really are. Be honest in your evaluation of yourselves, measuring yourselves by the faith God has given us. Just as our bodies have many parts and each part has a special function, so it is with Christ's body. We are many parts of one body, and we all belong to each other."

"In His grace, God has given us different gifts for doing certain things well. So if God has given you the ability to prophesy, speak out with as much faith as God has given you. If your gift is serving others, serve them well. If you are a teacher, teach well. If your gift is to encourage others, be encouraging. If it is giving, give generously. If God has given you leadership ability, take the responsibility seriously. And if you have a gift for showing kindness to others, do it gladly."

"Don't just pretend to love others. Really love them. Hate what is wrong. Hold tightly to what is good. Love each other with genuine affection and take delight in honoring each other. Never be lazy but work hard and serve the LORD enthusiastically. Rejoice in our confident hope. Be patient in trouble and keep on praying. When God's people are in need, be ready to help them. Always be eager to practice hospitality."

"Bless those who persecute you. Don't curse them; pray that God will bless them. Be happy with those who are happy, and weep with those who weep. Live in harmony with each other. Don't be too proud to enjoy the company of ordinary people. And don't think you know it all!"

"Never pay back evil with more evil. Do things in such a way that everyone can see you are honorable. Do all that you can to live in peace with everyone. Dear friends, never take revenge. Leave that to the righteous anger of God." For the Scriptures say,

> 'I will take revenge; I will pay them back,' says the LORD. Instead, 'If your enemies are hungry, feed them. If they are thirsty, give them something to drink. In doing this, you will heap burning coals of shame on their heads.'

"Don't let evil conquer you but conquer evil by doing good." (Romans 12).

Romans 12 gives a lot of sound instruction in how to live in the coming days. We cannot be lazy, there is too much work to do. We are all part of one body, and we need each other. This is what real love looks like. Love gives and gives and gives and gives. Love thinks of others as more important than we are. Love always looks after the needs of others, even those who hate us. In the coming days, we will spend our time and energy and resources loving others.

I think this is going to be hard. There is no way we can ever do this on our own, so God in His mercy has given us a NEW WAY.

4 THE NEW WAY

God knew that man could never love like this on his own. It is not possible, so He made a new way. The new way to get to God, who is Love, is to go through Jesus. Jesus told him, "I am the way, the truth, and the life. No one can come to the Father except through Me." (John 14:6). The only way to get to the Father is to go through Jesus.

"The old way, with laws etched in stone, led to death, though it began with such glory that the people of Israel could not bear to look at Moses' face. For his face shone with the glory of God, even though the brightness was already fading away. Shouldn't we expect far greater glory under the new way, now that the Holy Spirit is giving life? If the old way, which brings condemnation, was glorious, how much more glorious is the new way, which makes us right with God! In fact, that first glory was not glorious at all compared with the overwhelming glory of the new way. So if the old way, which has been replaced, was glorious, how much more glorious is the new, which remains forever!"

"Since this new way gives us such confidence, we can be very bold. We are not like Moses, who put a veil over his face so the people of Israel would not see the glory, even though it was destined to fade away. But the people's minds were hardened, and to this day whenever the old covenant is being read, the same veil covers their minds so they cannot understand the truth. And this veil can be removed only by believing in Christ. Yes, even today when they read Moses' writings, their hearts are covered with that veil, and they do not understand." (2 Corinthians 3:7-15). The old way, which had to do with keeping the law, did not work.

Instead, it brought condemnation. Our hearts are hardened, and a veil covers our minds so that we cannot understand the truth.

But with the new way, "You have died with Christ, and He has set you free from the spiritual powers of this world. So why do you keep on following the rules of the world, such as, "Don't handle! Don't taste! Don't touch!?" Such rules are mere human teachings about things that deteriorate as we use them. These rules may seem wise because they require strong devotion, pious self-denial, and severe bodily discipline. But they provide no help in conquering a person's evil desires." (Colossians 2:20-23). Following laws and rules will do nothing to help us conquer our evil desires. Following Jesus is more than just following rules. We must conquer our evil desires. But how?

"Since you have been raised to new life with Christ, set your sights on the realities of heaven, where Christ sits in the place of honor at God's right hand. Think about the things of heaven, not the things of earth. For you died to this life, and your real life is hidden with Christ in God. And when Christ, who is your life, is revealed to the whole world, you will share in all His glory." (Colossians 3:1-4). We must let the Spirit change our thoughts and our attitudes. We do this by setting our sights on the realities of heaven. Heaven is what is real. God is real. Jesus is real. LOVE is real. We think about these things. Our REAL LIFE is hidden with Christ in God. Meditate on that one for a while. And one day when Christ – who is our life – is revealed to the whole world, we will share in all His glory. That is insane. So how does this new way work?

"But whenever someone turns to the Lord, the veil is taken away. For the Lord is the Spirit, and wherever the Spirit of the Lord is, there is freedom. So all of us who have had that veil removed can see and reflect the glory of the Lord. And the Lord – who is the Spirit – makes us more and more like Him as we are changed into His glorious image." (2 Corinthians 3:16-18). Oh, my goodness! All we have to do is keep turning to Jesus; He does the rest. He removes the veil, and then He then sets us free from everything that gets in the way of us loving people and obeying God. We can then see and reflect His glory. Wow!

The glory of Jesus Christ Himself. Then we can really love people because Jesus really loved people.

"Therefore, since God in His mercy has given us this NEW WAY, we never give up. We reject all shameful deeds and underhanded methods. We don't try to trick anyone or distort the Word of God. We tell the truth before God, and all who are honest know this." (2 Corinthians 4:1). In His mercy God has given this new way – we turn to Jesus so that the veil will be removed, and we can find freedom. We keep turning to Jesus. No matter what happens, we turn to Jesus and tell the truth. We don't distort the Word of God. We embrace it. We love it. We live it. AND WE NEVER GIVE UP!

"You see, we don't go around preaching about ourselves. We preach that Jesus Christ is Lord, and we ourselves are your servants for Jesus' sake. For God, who said, 'Let there be light in the darkness,' has made this light shine in our hearts so we could know the glory of God that is seen in the face of Jesus Christ."

"We now have this light shining in our hearts, but we ourselves are like fragile clay jars containing this great treasure. This makes it clear that our great power is from God, not from ourselves." (2 Corinthians 4:5-7). Everything is Jesus. It is not us. We are just fragile clay jars, but we hold a treasure inside of us – LIGHT and LOVE. Jesus! Jesus is light. Jesus is love.

"Dear friends, I am not writing a new commandment for you; rather it is an old one you have had from the very beginning. This old commandment – to love one another – is the same message you heard before. Yet it is also new. Jesus lived the truth of this commandment, and you also are living it. For the darkness is disappearing, and the true light is already shining."

"If anyone claims, 'I am living in the light,' but hates his brother, that person is still living in darkness. Anyone who loves his brother is living in the light and does not cause others to stumble. But anyone who hates his brother is still living and walking in darkness. Such a person does not know the way to go, having been blinded by the darkness." (1 John 2:7-11).

The glory of God is seen in the face of Jesus Christ. As we continue turning to Jesus, the veil is removed, and we find freedom so that we can reflect the glory of God that is found in His Son. We then begin to love people – really love them.

Know this, the coming days are going to be hard. When God pours out His wrath on the earth, this place will be filled with every demon and every foul spirit. Whatever spirit is in a person will come to the surface. In the middle of the hatred and rage and lawlessness, love will shine brightly, and God will be highly exalted. That's why Paul wrote, "We are pressed on every side by troubles, but we are not crushed. We are perplexed, but not driven to despair. We are hunted down, but never abandoned by God. We get knocked down, but we are not destroyed. Through suffering, our bodies continue to share in the death of Jesus so that the life of Jesus may be seen in our bodies."

"Yes, we live under constant danger of death because we serve Jesus, so that the life of Jesus will be evident in our dying bodies. So we live in the face of death, but this has resulted in eternal life for you."

"But we continue to preach because we have the same kind of faith the psalmist had when he said, 'I believed in God, so I spoke.' We know that God, who raised the Lord Jesus, will also raise us with Jesus and present us to Himself together with you. All of this is for your benefit. And as God's grace reaches more and more people, there will be great thanksgiving, and God will receive more and more glory."

"That is why we never give up. Though our bodies are dying, our spirits are being renewed every day. For our present troubles are small and won't last very long. Yet they produce for us a glory that vastly outweighs them and will last forever! So we don't look at the troubles we can see now; rather, we fix our gaze on things that cannot be seen.

For the things we see now will soon be gone, but the things we cannot see will last forever." (2 Corinthians 4:8-18).

No matter what happens, we turn to Jesus. He will remove the veil so that we can find freedom. The Spirit will then change our thoughts and attitudes, then we can see and reflect His glory. We will be like Jesus on this earth. Jesus is the exact reflection of perfect love – God.

This perfect love will not be easy; it will cost us everything. Look at what it cost Jesus. But these troubles will not last long, and they will produce in us a glory that will last forever. This is God's big, good plan. It is a plan to prosper and not to harm, a plan to give hope and a future. Jesus is the only way to get to perfect love. He is the NEW WAY. If we keep turning to Him, He will lead us straight into the arms of His Father, who is perfect love.

5 THE HIGH COST OF FOLLOWING JESUS.

How can we possibly love like God loves? God's love is genuine, sincere, unfailing, and never ending. But more than that, God's love is sacrificial. It cost Him everything. When we think of love, we think of what we get, but when God thinks of love, He thinks about what we give. To love like God is asking us to love will cost us everything. We will have to die to self to live for God.

Just before His death Jesus said, "Now the time has come for the Son of Man to enter into His glory. I tell you the truth unless a kernel of wheat is planted in the soil and dies, it remains alone. But its death will produce many new kernels – a plentiful harvest of new lives. Those who love their life in this world will lose it. Those who care nothing for their life in this world will keep it for eternity. Anyone who wants to serve Me must follow Me, because My servants must be where I am. And the Father will honor anyone who serves Me." (John 12:23-26).

There is a high cost to following Jesus. In the coming days, it will cost us our hopes and our dreams, our money and resources, our time and energy, possibly our happiness, and maybe even our life. Look at what love cost Jesus. Look at what love cost the early church. If we love this life on earth, we will lose our real life. But if we care nothing for our life in this world, we will keep our real life for all of eternity.

"Look, I am sending you out as sheep among wolves. So be shrewd as snakes and harmless as doves. But beware! For you will be handed over to the courts and will be flogged with whips in the synagogues. You will stand trial before governors and kings because you are My followers. But this will be your opportunity to tell the rulers and other unbelievers about Me. When you are arrested, don't worry about how to respond or what to say. God will give you the right words at the right time. For it is not you who will be speaking – it will be the Spirit of your Father speaking through you."

"A brother will betray his brother to death, a father will betray his own child, and children will rebel against their parents and cause them to be killed. And all nations will hate you because you are My followers. But EVERYONE WHO ENDURES TO THE END will be saved. When you are persecuted in one town, flee to the next. I tell you the truth, the Son of Man will return before you have reached all the towns of Israel."

"Students are not greater than their teacher, and slaves are not greater than their master. Students are to be like their teacher, and slaves are to be like their master. And since I, the Master of the household, have been called the prince of demons, the members of My household will be called by even worse names!"

"But don't be afraid of those who threaten you. For the time is coming when everything that is covered will be revealed, and all that is secret will be made known to all. What I tell you now in the darkness, shout abroad when daybreak comes. What I whisper in your ear, shout from the housetops for all to hear!'

"Don't be afraid of those who want to kill your body, they cannot touch your soul. Fear only God, who can destroy both soul and body in hell. What is the price of two sparrows – one copper coin? But not a single sparrow can fall to the ground without your Father knowing it. And the very hairs on your head are all numbered. So don't be afraid; you are more valuable to God than a whole flock of sparrows."

"Everyone who acknowledges Me publicly here on earth, I will also acknowledge before My Father in heaven. But everyone who denies Me here on earth, I will also deny before My Father in heaven."

"Don't imagine that I came to bring peace to the earth! I came not to bring peace, but a sword.

> 'I have come to set a man against his father, a daughter against her mother, and a daughter-in-law against her mother-in-law. Your enemies will be right in your own household!'

"If you love your father or mother more than you love Me, you are not worthy of being mine; or if you love your son or daughter more than Me, you are not worthy of being mine. If you refuse to take up your cross and follow Me, you are not worthy of being mine. If you cling to your life, you will lose it, but if you give up your life for Me, you will find it." (Matthew 10:16-39).

According to this passage in Matthew, we can see that it will not be easy to love, but we cannot let our heart turn against the one who wants to harm us.

"But to you who are willing to listen, I say, love your enemies! Do good to those who hate you. Bless those who curse you. Pray for those who hurt you. If someone slaps you on one cheek, offer the other cheek also. If someone demands your coat, offer your shirt also. Give to anyone who asks; and when things are taken away from you, don't try to get them back. Do to others as you would like them to do to you."

"If you love only those who love you, why should you get credit for that? Even sinners love those who love them! And if you do good only to those who do good to you, why should you get credit? Even sinners do that much! And if you lend money only to those who can repay you, why should you get credit? Even sinners lend to other sinners for a full return."

"Love your enemies! Do good to them. Lend to them without expecting to be repaid. Then your reward from heaven will be very great, and you will truly be acting as children of the Most High, for He is kind to those who are unthankful and wicked. You must be compassionate, just as your Father is compassionate." (Luke 6:27-36).

It is impossible to do what God is asking us to do and still be connected to this world and all that it has to offer. We must throw off our old sinful nature and our former way of life, which is corrupted by lust and deception. Instead, we must let the Spirit renew our thoughts and attitudes. We must put on our new nature, created to be LIKE GOD – truly righteous and holy. (Ephesians 4:22-24).

Our old sinful nature is very selfish and self-seeking. We are always looking for a return on our investment. Our new nature, created to be like God, is always looking to give and serve and help. Our new nature can see past what is being done and see a real person who God loves. Our new nature can sincerely want freedom and deliverance for that person who wants to kill us. Our new nature is merciful and compassionate. To do what God is asking us to do, we must take off the old and put on the new. We must let the Spirit renew our thoughts and attitudes. We must take every thought captive to the obedience of Christ Jesus. We must learn to know our Creator so that we can become like Him – truly righteous and holy. God is love, and love is all that counts.

"If I could speak all the languages of earth and of angels, but didn't love others, I would only be a noisy gong or a clanging cymbal. If I had the gift of prophecy, and if I understood all of God's secret plans and possessed all knowledge, and if I had such faith that I could move mountains, but didn't love others, I would be nothing. If I gave everything I have to the poor and even sacrificed my body, I could boast about it but if I didn't love others, I would have gained nothing."

"Love is patient and kind. Love is not jealous or boastful or proud or rude. It does not demand its own way. It is not irritable, and it keeps no record of being wronged. It does not rejoice about injustice but rejoices whenever the truth wins out.

>Love never gives up,

>never loses faith,

is always hopeful,

and endures through every circumstance."

"Prophecy and speaking in unknown languages and special knowledge will become useless. But love will last forever! Now our knowledge is partial and incomplete, and even the gift of prophecy reveals only part of the whole picture! But when the time of perfection comes, these partial things will become useless." (1 Corinthians 13:1-10).

I believe that the time of perfection has come. God is pouring out His favor on His people, and we will all be able to walk in this kind of love in the coming days. This is the new way. LOVE. And it comes with a high cost.

PERFECT LOVE IS THE NARROW WAY THAT LEADS TO LIFE

The golden rule says to do unto others what you would want them to do unto you. This is the narrow way that leads to life. I want to give you the whole passage.

"Do to others whatever you would like them to do to you. This is the essence of all that is taught in the law and the prophets. You can enter God's Kingdom only through the narrow gate (to treat others like you would want to be treated). The highway to hell is broad, and its gate is wide for the many who choose that way. But the gateway to life is very narrow and the road is difficult (perfect love), and only a few ever find it." (Matthew 7:12-14). If this were not warning enough, it goes on.

"Beware of false prophets who come disguised as harmless sheep but are really vicious wolves. You can identify them by their fruit, that is, by the way they act. Can you pick grapes from thornbushes, or figs from thistles? A good tree produces good fruit, and a bad tree produces bad fruit. A good tree can't produce bad fruit, and a bad tree can't produce good fruit. So every tree that does not produce good fruit is chopped down and thrown into the fire. Yes, just as you can identify a tree by its fruit, so you can identify people by their actions." (Matthew 7:15-20).

Oh, my goodness. If we are not treating others like we would want to be treated, we are just a vicious wolf in sheep's clothing. We are a bad tree that produces bad fruit. This tree will be chopped down and thrown into the fire. God is telling His people what He expects. If we cannot learn to love people like He loves them, we are on the broad road that leads to destruction.

"Not everyone who calls out to Me, 'Lord, Lord!' will enter the Kingdom of Heaven. Only those who actually do the will of My Father in heaven will enter. On judgment day many will say to Me, 'Lord, Lord!' 'We prophesied in Your name and cast out demons in Your name and performed many miracles in Your name.'" But I will reply, 'I never knew you. Get away from Me, you who break God's laws.' (Matthew 7:21-23). Only those who actually do the will of our Father in heaven will enter the Kingdom of Heaven. God's will is that we love one another.

"Anyone who listens to My teaching and follows it is wise, like a person who builds a house on solid rock. Though the rain comes in torrents and the floodwaters rise and the winds beat against that house, it won't collapse because it is built on bedrock. But anyone who hears My teaching and doesn't obey it is foolish, like a person who builds a house on sand. When the rains and floods come and the winds beat against that house, it will collapse with a mighty crash." (Matthew 7:24-27).

In the coming days the rain will come in torrents, and the floodwaters will rise. Only those who listen and obey the words of this teaching will make it. Their houses will stand. The other houses will fall.

SEPERATING THE SHEEP FROM THE GOATS

If the passage in Matthew 7 was not enough to convince us, Jesus tells us about the final judgment in Matthew 25:31-46.

"But when the Son of Man comes in His glory, and all the angels with Him, then He will sit upon His glorious throne. All the nations will be gathered in His presence, and He will separate the people as a shepherd separates the sheep from the goats. He will place the sheep at His right hand and the goats at His left."

"Then the King will say to those on His right, 'Come, you who are blessed by My Father, inherit the Kingdom prepared for you from the creation of the world. For I was hungry, and you fed Me. I was thirsty, and you gave Me a drink. I was a stranger, and you invited Me into your home. I was naked, and you gave Me clothing. I was sick, and you cared for Me. I was in prison, and you visited Me.'

"Then these righteous ones will reply, 'Lord, when did we ever see You hungry and feed You? Or thirsty and give You something to drink? Or a stranger and show You hospitality? Or naked and give You clothing? When did we ever see You sick or in prison and visit You?'

And the King will say, 'I tell you the truth, when you did it to one of the least of these My brothers, you were doing it to Me!'" Wow! Jesus so identifies with people – all people – that He considers how we are treating others to be how we are treating Him. If we are kind to people, we are kind to Jesus. That is crazy.

"Then the King will turn to those on the left and say, 'Away with you, you cursed ones, into the eternal fire prepared for the devil and his demons. For I was hungry, and you didn't feed Me. I was thirsty, and you didn't give Me a drink. I was a stranger, and you didn't invite Me into your home. I was naked, and you didn't give Me clothing. I was sick and in prison, and you didn't visit Me.'

"Then they will reply, 'Lord, when did we ever see You hungry or thirsty, or a stranger or naked or sick or in prison, and not help You?'

"And He will answer, 'I tell you the truth, when you refused to help the least of these My brothers, you were refusing to help Me.'

"And they will go away into eternal punishment, but the righteous will go into eternal life."

There is a high cost to following Jesus. It will cost us everything, but we will get so much more in return. Eternal life. There is a much higher cost to not following Jesus. Eternal punishment. The choice is ours.

6 HOW DOES GOD LOVE HIS PEOPLE?

God disciplines those He loves. I know no one wants to talk about the discipline of God, but we must. The same storm that is coming upon the whole world will hit our house too. We must talk about what to do when the storm hits.

First, know that this is God's plan. It is a plan that He had from the foundation of the world, and it is a plan to prosper and not to harm. This is what the LORD says: "You will be in Babylon for seventy years. But then I will come and do for you all the good things I have promised, and I will bring you home again. For I know the plans I have for you," says the LORD. "They are plans for good and not for disaster, to give you a future and a hope. In those days when you pray, I will listen. If you look for Me WHOLEHEARTEDLY, you will find Me. I will be found by you," says the LORD. "I will end your captivity and restore your fortunes. I will gather you out of the nations where I sent you and will bring you home again to your own land." (Jeremiah 29:10-14).

God is after our heart – our whole heart. Everything that happens – every circumstance – is designed to turn our hearts toward Jesus so that He can heal us and set us free, so that He can do some kind thing for us. It is only when we are healed and delivered that we can truly be free to know God. "And we know that God causes everything to work together for the good of those who love God and are called according to His purpose for them. For God knew His people in advance, and He chose them to become like His Son, so that His Son would be the firstborn among many brothers and sisters. And having chosen them, He called them to come to Him. And having called them, He gave them right standing with Himself. And having given them right standing, He gave them His glory." (Romans 8:28-30).

Everything that is about to happen will turn out for our good. In the coming days, we will be conformed into the image of Christ. He has chosen us, and He is calling us to come to Him. No matter what happens, we will turn to Jesus, and He will make us right with Himself, and He then will give us His glory. That is crazy. Jesus will do it all. All we have to do is turn to Him.

Hebrews 11 talks about those people who went before us, those who showed us the way. They, too, had it hard. "By faith these people overthrew kingdoms, ruled with justice, and received what God had promised them. They shut the mouths of lions, quenched the flames of fire, and escaped death by the edge of the sword. Their weakness was turned to strength. They became strong in battle and put whole armies to flight. Women received their loved ones back again from death."

"But others were tortured, refusing to turn from God in order to be set free. They placed their hope in a better life after the resurrection. Some were jeered at, and their backs were cut open with whips. Others were chained in prisons. Some died by stoning, some were sawed in half, and others were killed with the sword. Some went about wearing skins of sheep and goats, destitute and oppressed and mistreated. They were too good for this world, wandering over deserts and mountains, hiding in caves and holes in the ground."

"All these people earned a good reputation because of their faith, yet none of them received all that God had promised. For God had something better in mind for us, so that they would not reach perfection without us." (Hebrews 11:33-40).

All these people were people of faith. Look at what they went through. None of them had it easy, yet all of them earned a good reputation. But somehow or another, their faith will not reach perfection without us. I believe that each generation carried a baton and passed it to the next generation until the last generation crosses the finish line. I believe that we are in the last lap. We will cross the finish line as a bride fully prepare to meet her groom. We could not have done it without them.

"Therefore, since we are surrounded by such a huge crowd of witnesses to the life of faith, let us strip off every weight that slows us down, especially the sin that so easily trips us up. And let us run with endurance the race God has set before us. We do this by keeping our eyes on Jesus, the champion who initiates and perfects our faith." (Hebrews 12:1-2).

Every one of us has a race set before us that we must run. Some races are hard. Some races are long. Some are long and hard. Some are just sprints. But whatever race God sets before us, it can only be run if our eyes are fixed on Jesus. He started this race, and He will finish it if we keep our eyes on Him to the end.

"Because of the joy awaiting Him, Jesus endured the cross, disregarding its shame. Now He is seated in the place of honor beside God's throne. Think of all the hostility He endured from sinful people, then you won't become weary and give up. After all, you have not yet given your lives in your struggle against sin." (Hebrews 12:2-4). In the coming days, our struggle will be against sin. We will want to turn against people. We will want to give up and give in, but we can't. We must keep going. We must make it to the finish line with our eyes still firmly fixed on Jesus. We can't give up.

"And have you forgotten the encouraging words God spoke to you as His children? He said,

> 'My child, don't make light of the LORD's discipline, and don't give up when He corrects you. For the LORD disciplines those He loves, and He punishes each one He accepts as His child.'

"As you endure this divine discipline, remember that God is treating you as His own children. Who ever heard of a child who is never disciplined by its father? If God doesn't discipline you as He does all of His children, it means that you are illegitimate and are not really His children at all. Since we respected our earthly fathers who disciplined us, shouldn't we submit even more to the discipline of the Father of our spirits, and live forever?"

"For our earthly fathers disciplined us for a few years, doing the best they knew how. But God's discipline is always good for us, so that we might share in His holiness. No discipline is enjoyable while it is happening – it's painful! But afterward there will be a peaceful harvest of right living for those who are trained in this way."

"So take a new grip with your tired hands and strengthen your weak knees. Mark out a straight path for your feet so that those who are weak and lame will not fall but become strong." (Hebrews 12:5-13).

We must get rid of the sin that is inside of us. God will stay with us until we do. The coming hardship is a kindness that will lead to repentance. It won't feel good, but it will be good. Holiness will be the result.

"So work at living in peace with everyone, and work at living a holy life, for those who are not holy will not see the Lord. Look after each other so that none of you fails to receive the grace of God. Watch out that no poisonous root of bitterness grows up to trouble you, corrupting many. Make sure that no one is immoral or godless like Esau, who traded his birthright as the firstborn son for a single meal. You know that afterward, when he wanted his father's blessing, he was rejected. It was too late for repentance, even though he begged with bitter tears." (Hebrews 12:14-17).

We must take every hardship as discipline from God. We must guard and value everything we have so that we won't lose it like Esau did. We must protect our heart and protect the hearts of others in the coming days. But know this, we have not come to a harsh place.

"You have not come to a physical mountain, to a place of flaming fire, darkness, gloom, and whirlwind, as the Israelites did at Mount Sinai. For they heard an awesome trumpet blast and a voice so terrible that they begged God to stop speaking. They staggered back under God's command: 'If even an animal touches the mountain, it must be stoned to death.' Moses himself was so frightened at the sight that he said, 'I am terrified and trembling.'" (Hebrews 12:18-21).

"No, you have come to Mount Zion, to the city of the living God, the heavenly Jerusalem, and to countless thousands of angels in a joyful gathering. You have come to the assembly of God's firstborn children, whose names are written in heaven. You have come to God Himself, who is the judge over all things. You have come to the spirits of the righteous ones in heaven who have now been made perfect. You have come to Jesus, the One who mediates the new covenant between God and people, and to the sprinkled blood, which speaks of forgiveness instead of crying out for vengeance like the blood of Able."

"Be careful that you do not refuse to listen to the One who is speaking. For if the people of Israel did not escape when they refused to listen to Moses, the earthly messenger, we will certainly not escape if we reject the One who speaks to us from heaven! When God spoke from Mount Sinai His voice shook the earth, but now He makes another promise: 'Once again I will shake not only the earth but the heavens also.' This means that all of creation will be shaken and removed, so that only unshakable things will remain."

"Since we are receiving a Kingdom that is unshakeable, let us be thankful and please God by worshiping Him with holy fear and awe. For our God is a devouring fire." (Hebrews 12:22-29).

In the coming days everything that can be shaken will be shaken. This shaking will either refine or destroy all the inhabitants of the earth. The time of God's judgment has come, but this is also the time of His favor. This favor will teach us to trust Jesus and to love people. In the coming days, God will put us all to the test. Do you trust Me? Do you love Me? Then love people. Trust it! Everything that is about to happen is for our good and God's glory. Fix your eyes on Jesus, guard your heart, and give thanks. God is always up to something good, and this is His hour.

DO NOT IGNORE THE OBSTACLES

I must add one more thing to this chapter because God keeps bringing it to my attention. Don't ignore the obstacles. There are going to be things that God puts in our way in the coming days that are meant to turn us in another direction. Don't ignore them. There will be huge consequences if we do.

"Son of man, I have appointed you as a watchman for Israel. Whenever you receive a message from Me, warn the people immediately. If I warn the wicked, saying, 'You are under the penalty of death,' but you fail to deliver the warning, they will die in their sins. And I will hold you responsible for their deaths. If you warn them and they refuse to repent and keep on sinning, they will die in their sins. But you will have saved yourself because you obeyed Me."

"If righteous people turn away from their righteous behavior and ignore the obstacles I put in their way, they will die. And if you do not warn them, they will die in their sins. None of their righteous acts will be remembered, and I will hold you responsible for their deaths. But if you warn righteous people not to sin and they listen to you and do not sin, they will live, and you will have saved yourself, too." (Ezekiel 3:17-21).

If righteous people, that's us if we are wanting to follow hard after God, turn from their righteous behavior. It sounds like there might be times when we want to do something other than what is right, and we might not even know that it is not right. God will not let us. He will put obstacles in our way. Hallelujah, thank you Jesus! But if we ignore those obstacles, we will die in our sins and none of our righteous acts will be remembered anymore. This is serious, but God is not going to let us leave the path of righteousness. He is going to continually redirect us until we get it right. Trust it. Pay attention. If things get hard, if there is a roadblock in every direction you turn, if people keep saying, "No," listen. We only think we know where we are going, but God is ordering

What does God's favor look like?

our footsteps.

32

7 WHAT DOES THIS DIVINE DISCIPLINE LOOK LIKE?

When I think about what divine discipline looks like, I must go to the Bible and look at the people God loved. What happened to them? God oftentimes had to use extreme measures to get their attention and get the results He wanted. But know this, God will not allow anything to happen to us that is not absolutely necessary. Trust it. God has a good plan for each of us, a plan to prosper and not to harm, a plan to give us hope and a future, and He will use hardships to discipline those He loves. Everything that happens to us is designed to take us to Jesus and to a place of holiness in the LORD.

JEREMIAH

Jeremiah was a man chosen by God. Jeremiah 1 records: The LORD gave me this message, "I knew you before I formed you in your mother's womb. Before you were born, I set you apart and appointed you as My prophet to the nations."

"O Sovereign LORD," I said, "I can't speak for You! I'm too young!" The LORD replied, "Don't say, 'I'm too young,' for you must go wherever I send you and say whatever I tell you. And don't be afraid of the people, for I will be with you and will protect you. I, the LORD, have spoken!" Then the LORD reached out and touched my mouth and said,

"Look, I have put My words in your mouth! Today I appoint you to stand up against nations and kingdoms. Some you must uproot and tear down, destroy and overthrow. Others you must build up and plant." (Jeremiah 1:3-10).

Jeremiah was highly called and chosen. He was used by God in mighty ways to build up and to tear down, but God had to discipline this mighty man of God. Jeremiah wrote about it in Lamentations 3.

"I am the one who has seen the afflictions that come from the rod of the LORD's anger. He has led me into darkness, shutting out all light. He has turned His hand against me again and again, all day long."

"He has made my skin and flesh grow old. He has broken my bones. He has besieged and surrounded me with anguish and distress. He has buried me in the dark place like those long dead."

"He has walled me in, and I cannot escape. He has bound me in heavy chains. And though I cry and shout, He has shut out my prayers. He has blocked my way with a high stone wall; He has made my road crooked."

"He has hidden like a bear or a lion, waiting to attack me. He has dragged me off the path and torn me in pieces, leaving me helpless and devastated. He has drawn His bow and made me the target for His arrows."

"He shot His arrows deep into my heart. My own people laugh at me. All day long they sing their mocking songs. He has filled me with bitterness and given me a bitter cup of sorrow to drink."

"He has made me chew on gravel. He has rolled me in the dust. Peace has been stripped away, and I have forgotten what prosperity is. I cry out, "My splendor is gone! Everything I had hoped for from the LORD is lost."

"The thought of my suffering and homelessness is bitter beyond words. I will never forget this awful time, as I grieve over my loss." (Lamentations 3:1-20).

This is God's discipline. He is trying to turn Jeremiah's heart back to Himself. He is showing Jeremiah that his actions or attitudes are not in line with His. Jeremiah never questioned where these hardships came from. He knew. Then he goes on to write...

Yet I still dare to hope when I remember this:

"The faithful love of the LORD never ends! His mercies never cease. Great is His faithfulness; His mercies begin afresh each morning. I say to myself, 'The LORD is my inheritance; therefore, I will hope in Him!'"

"The LORD is good to those who depend on Him, to those who search for Him. So it is good to wait quietly for salvation from the LORD. And it is good for people to submit at an early age to the yoke of His discipline:

"Let them sit alone in silence beneath the LORD's demands. Let them lie face down in the dust, for there may be hope at last. Let them turn the other cheek to those who strike them and accept the insults of their enemies."

"For no one is abandoned by the LORD forever. Though He brings grief, He also shows compassion because of the greatness of His unfailing love. For He does not enjoy hurting people or causing them sorrow." (Lamentations 3:21-33).

Listen to what Jeremiah is saying. He remembers who God is. He knows his God. He knows that He is merciful and compassionate and faithful. His hope is in God, so He sits alone in silence beneath the LORD's demands.

"If people crush underfoot all the prisoners of the land, if they deprive others of their rights in defiance of the Most High, if they twist justice in the courts – doesn't the LORD see all these things?"

"Who can command things to happen without the LORD's permission? Does not the Most High send both calamity and good? Then why should we, mere humans complain when we are punished for our sins?"

"Instead, let us test and examine our ways. Let us turn back to the LORD. Let us lift our hearts and hands to God in heaven and say, 'We have sinned and rebelled, and You have not forgiven us.'" (Lamentations 3:34-42).

DAVID

"O LORD, don't rebuke me in Your anger or discipline me in Your rage! Your arrows have struck deep, and Your blows are crushing me. Because of Your anger, my whole body is sick; my health is broken because of my sins. My guilt overwhelms me – it is a burden too heavy to bear. My wounds fester and stink because of my foolish sins. I am bent over and racked with pain. All day long I walk around filled with grief. A raging fever burns within me, and my health is broken. I am exhausted and completely crushed. My groans come from an anguished heart."

"You know what I long for, LORD; You hear my every sigh. My heart beats wildly, my strength fails, and I am going blind. My loved ones and friends stay away, fearing my disease. Even my own family stands at a distance. Meanwhile, my enemies lay traps to kill me. Those who wish me harm make plans to ruin me. All day long they plan their treachery."

"But I am silent before them as one who cannot speak. I choose to hear nothing, and I make no reply. For I am waiting for You, O LORD. You must answer for me, O Lord my God. I prayed, 'Don't let my enemies gloat over me or rejoice at my downfall.'"

"I am on the verge of collapse, facing constant pain. But I confess my sins; I am deeply sorry for what I have done. I have many aggressive enemies; they hate me without reason. They repay me evil for good and oppose me for pursuing good."

"Do not abandon me, O LORD. Do not stand at a distance, my God. Come quickly to help me, O Lord my Savior." (Psalm 38).

I said to myself, "I will watch what I do and not sin in what I say. I will hold my tongue when the ungodly are around me." But as I stood there in silence – not even speaking of good things – the turmoil within me grew worse. The more I thought about it, the hotter I got, igniting a fire of words. (Psalm 39:1-3).

In his own strength, David could not stop the sin that was within him.

"LORD, remind me how brief my time on earth will be. Remind me that my days are numbered – how fleeting my life is. You have made my life no longer than the width of my hand. My entire lifetime is just a moment to You; at best, each of us is but a breath."

"We are merely moving shadows, and all our busy rushing ends in nothing. We heap up wealth, not knowing who will spend it. And so, Lord, where do I put my hope? My only hope is in You. Rescue me from my rebellion." (Psalm 39:4-8).

Our only hope is in Jesus. Lord, rescue us from our rebellion!

"I am silent before You: I won't say a word, for my punishment is from You. But please stop striking me! I am exhausted by the blows from Your hand. When you discipline us for our sins, You consume like a moth what is precious to us. Each of us is but a breath."

"Hear my prayer, O LORD! Listen to my cries for help! Don't ignore my tears. For I am Your guest – a traveler passing through, as my ancestors were before me. Leave me alone so I can smile again before I am gone and exist no more." (Psalm 39:9-13).

This does not sound like it is fun, but David, a man after God's own heart, kept turning to God. No matter what happened, he turned to God. God is the only One who can rescue us. Then Psalm 40 goes on to say...

"I waited patiently for the LORD to help me, and He turned to me and heard my cry. He lifted me out of the pit of despair, out of the mud and the mire. He set my feet on solid ground and steadied me as I walked along. He has given me a new song to sing, a hymn of praise to our God. Many will see what He has done and be amazed. They will put their trust in the LORD."

"Oh, the joys of those who trust the LORD, who have no confidence in the proud or in those who worship idols. O LORD my God, You have performed many wonders for us. Your plans for us are too numerous to list. You have no equal. If I tried to recite all Your wonderful deeds, I would never come to the end of them."

"You take no delight in sacrifices or offerings. NOW THAT YOU HAVE MADE ME LISTEN, I FINALLY UNDERSTAND – You don't require burnt offerings or sin offerings. Then I said, 'Look, I have come. As is written about me in the Scriptures: I take joy in doing Your will, my God for Your instructions are written on my heart.'" (Psalm 40:1-8).

God is about to make all of us understand. He will write His instructions on our heart, and we will take joy in doing His will.

"Oh, what joy for those whose disobedience is forgiven, whose sin is put out of sight! Yes, what joy for those whose record the LORD has cleared of guilt, whose lives are lived in COMPLETE HONESTY! When I refused to confess my sin, my body wasted away, and I groaned all day long. Day and night Your hand of discipline was heavy on me. My strength evaporated like water in the summer heat."

"Finally, I confessed all my sins to You and stopped trying to hide my guilt. I said to myself, 'I will confess my rebellion to the LORD.' And You forgave me! All my sin is gone." (Psalm 32:1-5).

God wants honesty – we must be honest with ourselves and be honest with Him. Then we can come to Him without excuse and confess our sins. Then He forgives us! What joy! All the discipline paid off. We are now free from sin. We are now free to worship Him.

"Therefore, let all the godly pray to You while there is still time, that they may not drown in the floodwaters of judgment. For You are my hiding place; You protect me from trouble. You surround me with songs of victory."

The LORD says, "I will guide you along the best pathway for your life. I will advise you and watch over you. Do not be like a senseless horse or mule that needs a bit and bridle to keep it under control."

"Many sorrows come to the wicked, but unfailing love surrounds those who trust the LORD. So rejoice in the LORD and be glad, all you who obey Him! Shout for joy, all you whose hearts are pure!" (Psalm 32:6-11).

God is looking for those who will obey Him with pure hearts. This divine discipline will give us both. Trust it. No matter how hard it gets, God has a good plan in it all.

JOB

No one wants to talk about Job because "he was blameless – a man of complete integrity. He feared God and stayed away from evil." (Job 1:1). But Job lost his children, his animals, his servants, and all his wealth in one day. In all of this, Job still did not sin by blaming God.

Then the LORD asked Satan, "Have you noticed my servant, Job? He is the finest man in all the earth. He is blameless – a man of complete integrity. He fears God and stays away from evil. And he has maintained his integrity, even though you URGED ME TO HARM HIM WITHOUT A CAUSE.' It was God who took all those things from Job, and it was God who took his health. He allowed it all to happen. Why?

By the time all his trials were over, Job replied to the LORD:

"I know that You can do anything, and no one can stop you. You asked, 'Who is this that questions My wisdom with such ignorance?'"

"It is I – and I was talking about things I knew nothing about, things far too wonderful for me. You said, 'Listen and I will speak! I have some questions for you, and you must answer them.'"

"I had only heard about You before, but now I have seen You with my own eyes. I take back everything I said, and I sit in dust and ashes to show my repentance." (Job 42:1-6).

I still don't know why Job had to go through all that he had to go through. What I do know is that Job came to know God in ways he had never known Him before. And whatever he learned from God caused him to repent in dust and ashes. The same thing will happen to us. In the coming days, we will know God in ways we never imagined, and we, too, will repent in sackcloth and ashes.

James 5 says:

"Dear brothers and sisters, be patient as you wait for the Lord's return. Consider the farmers who patiently wait for the rains in the fall and in the spring. They eagerly look for the valuable harvest to ripen. You, too, must be patient. Take courage, for the coming of the Lord is near."

"Don't grumble about each other, brothers and sisters, or you will be judged. For look – the Judge is standing at the door!"

"For examples of patience in suffering dear brothers and sisters, look at the prophets who spoke in the name of the Lord. We give great honor to those who endure under suffering. For instance, you know about Job, a man of great endurance. You can see how the Lord was kind to him at the end, for the Lord is full of tenderness and mercy." (James 5:7-11).

There is always an end intended by the Lord. Whatever Job went through increased his faith and his endurance.

"Dear brothers and sisters, when troubles of any kind come your way, consider it an opportunity for great joy. For you know that when your faith is tested, your endurance has a chance to grow. So let it grow, for when your endurance is fully developed, you will be PERFECT and complete, needing nothing." (James 1:2-4).

No matter what happens, consider it an opportunity for great joy. God will make our endurance perfect also. Fix your eyes on Jesus, guard your heart, and give thanks. God is ALWAYS up to something good.

8 BLESSINGS AND CURSES BOTH COME FROM GOD.

Blessings and curses are both very real. Look at your own life. Look at the lives of others. You can tell. If we obey God, God blesses us. If we disobey God, there are consequences. Deuteronomy 28-30 tells us exactly what God is going to do if we obey, and what He is going to do if we disobey.

Deuteronomy 28: "If you fully obey the LORD your God and carefully keep all His commands that I am giving you today, the LORD your God will set you high above all the nations of the world. You will experience all these blessings if you obey the LORD your God:

>Your towns and your fields
>
>>will be blessed.
>
>Your children and your crops
>
>>will be blessed.
>
>The offspring of your herds and flocks
>
>>will be blessed.
>
>Your fruit baskets and breadboards
>
>>will be blessed.
>
>Wherever you go and whatever you do,

you will be blessed."

"The LORD will conquer your enemies when they attack you. They will attack you from one direction, but they will scatter from you in seven! The LORD will guarantee a blessing on everything you do and will fill your storehouses with grain. The LORD your God will bless you in the land He is giving you."

"If you obey the commands of the LORD your God and walk in His ways, the LORD will establish you as His holy people as He swore He would do. Then all the nations of the world will see that you are a people claimed by the LORD, and they will stand in awe of you."

"The LORD will give you prosperity in the land He swore to your ancestors to give you, blessing you with many children, numerous livestock, and abundant crops. The LORD will send rain at the proper time from His rich treasury in the heavens and will bless all the work you do. You will lend to many nations, but you will never need to borrow from them. If you listen to these commands of the LORD your God that I am giving you today, and if you carefully obey them, the LORD will make you the head and not the tail, and you will always be on top and never at the bottom. You must not turn away from any of the commands I am giving you today, nor follow after other gods and worship them." (Deuteronomy 28:1-14)

This is what God's blessing looks like. Everything we touch prospers. Everywhere we go, we prosper. Everything we do prospers. We are blessed. The LORD Himself commands it.

"But if you refuse to listen to the LORD your God and do not obey all the commands and decrees I am giving you today all these curses will come and overwhelm you:

> Your towns and your fields
>
> will be cursed.

> Your fruit baskets and breadboards
>
> > will be cursed.
>
> Your children and your crops
>
> > will be cursed.
>
> The offspring of your herds and flocks
>
> > will be cursed.
>
> Wherever you go and whatever you do,
>
> > you will be cursed."

"The LORD Himself will send on you curses, confusion, and frustration in everything you do, until at last you are completely destroyed for doing evil and abandoning Me. The LORD will afflict you with diseases until none of you are left in the land you are about to enter and occupy. The LORD will strike you with wasting diseases, fever, and inflammation, with scorching heat and drought, and with blight and mildew. These disasters will pursue you until you die. The skies above will be as unyielding as bronze, and the earth beneath will be as hard as iron. The LORD will change the rain that falls on your land into powder, and dust will pour down from the sky until you are destroyed."

"The LORD will cause you to be defeated by your enemies. You will attack your enemies from one direction, but you will scatter from them in seven! You will be an object of horror to all the kingdoms of the earth. Your corpses will be food for all the scavenging birds and wild animals, and no one will be there to chase them away."

"The LORD will afflict you with the boils of Egypt and with tumors, scurvy, and the itch, from which you cannot be cured. The LORD will strike you with madness, blindness, and panic. You will grope around in broad daylight like a blind person groping in the darkness, but you will not find your way. You will be oppressed and robbed continually, and no one will come to save you."

"You will be engaged to a woman, but another man will sleep with her. You will build a house, but someone else will live in it. You will plant a vineyard, but you will never enjoy its fruit. Your ox will be butchered before your eyes, but you will not eat a single bite of the meat. Your donkey will be taken from you, never to be returned. Your sheep and your goats will be given to your enemies, and no one will be there to help you. You will watch as your sons and daughters are taken away as slaves. Your heart will break for them, but you won't be able to help them. A foreign nation you have never heard about will eat the crops you worked so hard to grow. You will suffer under the tragedy you see around you. The LORD will cover your knees and legs with incurable boils. In fact, you will be covered from head to foot."

"The LORD will exile you and your king to a nation unknown to you and your ancestors. There in exile you will worship gods of wood and stone! You will become an object of horror, ridicule, and mockery among all the nations to which the LORD sends you."

"You will plant much but harvest little, for locusts will eat your crops. You will plant vineyards and care for them, but you will not drink the wine or eat the grapes, for worms will destroy the vines. You will grow olive trees throughout your land, but you will never use the olive oil, for the fruit will drop before it ripens. You will have sons and daughters, but you will lose them, for they will be led away into captivity. Swarms of insects will destroy your trees and crops."

"The foreigners living among you will become stronger and stronger, while you become weaker and weaker. They will lend money to you, but you will not lend to them. They will be the head, and you will be the tail!"

"If you refuse to listen to the LORD your God and to obey the commands and decrees He has given you, all these curses will pursue and overtake you until you are destroyed. These horrors will serve as a sign and warning among you and your descendants forever. If you do not serve the LORD your God with joy and enthusiasm for the abundant benefits you have received, you will serve your enemies whom the LORD will send against you. You will be left hungry, thirsty, naked, and lacking in everything. The LORD will put an iron yoke on your neck, oppressing you harshly until He has destroyed you."

"The LORD will bring a distant nation against you from the end of the earth, and it will swoop down on you like a vulture. It is a nation whose language you do not understand, a fierce and heartless nation that shows no respect for the old and no pity for the young. Its armies will devour your livestock and crops, and you will be destroyed. They will leave you no grain, new wine, olive oil, calves, or lambs, and you will starve to death. They will attack your cities until all the fortified walls in your land – the walls you trusted to protect you – are knocked down. They will attack all the towns in the land the LORD your God has given you."

"The siege and terrible distress of the enemy's attack will be so severe that you will eat the flesh of your own sons and daughters, whom the LORD your God has given you. The most tenderhearted man among you will have no compassion for his own brother, his beloved wife, and his surviving children. He will refuse to share with them the flesh he is devouring – the flesh of one of his own children – because he has nothing else to eat during the siege and terrible distress that your enemy will inflict on all your towns. The most tender and delicate woman among you – so delicate she would not so much as touch the ground with her foot – will be selfish toward the husband she loves and toward her own son or daughter. She will hide from them the afterbirth and the new baby she has borne, so that she herself can secretly eat them. She will have nothing else to eat during the siege and terrible distress that your enemy will inflict on all your towns."

"If you refuse to obey all the words of instruction that are written in this book, and if you do not fear the glorious and awesome name of the LORD your God, then the LORD will overwhelm you and your children with indescribable plagues. These plagues will be intense and without relief. The LORD will afflict you with every sickness and plague there is, even those not mentioned in this Book of Instruction, until you are destroyed. Though you become as numerous as the stars in the sky, few of you will be left because you would not listen to the LORD your God."

"Just as the LORD has found great pleasure in causing you to prosper and multiply, the LORD will find pleasure in destroying you. You will be torn from the land you are about to enter and occupy. For the LORD will scatter you among all the nations from one end of the earth to the other. There you will worship foreign gods that neither you nor your ancestors have known, gods made of wood and stone! There among those nations you will find no peace or place to rest. And the LORD will cause your heart to tremble, your eyesight to fail, and your soul to despair. Your life will constantly hang in the balance. You will live night and day in fear, unsure if you will survive. In the morning you will say, 'If only it were night!' And in the evening, you will say, 'If only it were morning!' For you will be terrified by the awful horrors you see around you. Then the LORD will send you back to Egypt in ships, to a destination I promised you would never see again. There you will offer to sell yourselves to your enemies as slaves, but no one will buy you." (Deuteronomy 28:15-68).

God is not playing. Look at the progression of the curses. I tremble when I read this. This will happen if we refuse to obey God.

We know if we are blessed or if we are cursed. No one has to tell us. Blessings and curses both come from God. If we choose to obey Him, we find blessings. If we choose to disobey, we will experience the wrath of God that is being poured out on the whole earth. We get to choose. He does the rest. But listen to what God says in Deuteronomy 30.

"In the future, when you EXPERIENCE all these blessings and curses, I have listed for you, and when you are living among the nations to which the LORD your God has exiled you, TAKE TO HEART ALL THESE

INSTRUCTIONS. If at that time you and your children return to the LORD your God, and if you OBEY WITH ALL YOUR HEART and all your soul all the commands I have given you today, then the LORD your God will restore your fortunes. He will have mercy on you and gather you back from all the nations where He has scattered you. Even though you are banished to the ends of the earth, the LORD your God will gather you from there and bring you back again. (Did you hear that?) The LORD your God will return you to the land that belonged to your ancestors, and you will possess that land again. Then He will make you more prosperous and numerous than your ancestors!"

"The LORD your God will change your heart and the hearts of all your descendants, so that you will love Him with all your heart and soul and so you may live! The LORD your God will inflict all these curses on your enemies and on those who hate and persecute you. Then you will again obey the LORD and keep all His commands that I am giving you today." Listen to what He is saying. God is going to do it all!

"The LORD your God will then make you successful in everything you do. He will give you many children and numerous livestock, and He will cause your fields to produce abundant harvests, for the LORD will again delight in being good to you as He was to your ancestors. The LORD your God will delight in you if you obey His voice and keep the commands and decrees written in this Book of Instruction, and if you turn to the LORD your God with all your heart and soul."

"This command I am giving you today is not too difficult for you, and it is not beyond your reach. It is not kept in heaven, so distant that you must ask, 'Who will go up to heaven and bring it down so we can hear it and obey?' It is not kept beyond the sea, so far away that you must ask, 'Who will cross the sea to bring it to us so we can hear it and obey?' No, the message is very close at hand; it is on your lips and in your heart so that you can obey it."

"Now listen! Today I am giving you a choice between life and death, between prosperity and disaster. For I command you this day to love the LORD your God and to keep His commands, decrees, and regulations by walking in His ways. If you do this, you will live and multiply, and the LORD your God will bless you and the land you are about to enter and occupy."

"But if your heart turns away and you refuse to listen, and if you are drawn away to serve and worship other gods, then I warn you now that you will certainly be destroyed. You will not live a long, good life in the land you are crossing the Jordan to occupy."

"Today I have given you the choice between life and death, between blessings and curses. Now I call on heaven and earth to witness the choice you make. Oh, that you would choose life, so that you and your descendants might live! You can make this choice by loving the LORD your God, obeying Him, and committing yourself firmly to Him. This is the key to your life. And if you love and obey the LORD, you will live long in the land the LORD swore to give your ancestors Abraham, Isaac, and Jacob." (Deuteronomy 30).

The choice is ours. God wants our heart – all of it. If we give Him our heart, we get His blessings. Blessings and curses are both His to give. In the coming days, we will be blessed. We will come to obey God with our whole heart. God will make sure we do.

9. HOW TO FIND GOD'S FAVOR IN OUR FINANCES.

The time of the LORD's favor has come. Remember that as you read this chapter. Turn to the Lord and open your heart wide. "But whenever someone turns to the Lord, the veil is taken away. For the Lord is the Spirit, and wherever the Spirit of the Lord is, there is freedom. So all of us who have had that veil removed can see and reflect the glory of the Lord. And the Lord – who is the Spirit – makes us more and more like Him as we are changed into His glorious image. Therefore, since God in His mercy has given us this new way, we never give up." (2 Corinthians 3:16-18, 4:1).

"Since you have heard about Jesus and have learned the truth that comes from Him, throw off your old sinful nature and your former way of life, which is corrupted by lust and deception. Instead, let the Spirit renew your thoughts and attitudes. Put on your new nature, created to be like God – truly righteous and holy." (Ephesians 4:21-24). What is God like? God is love.

I wanted to start this chapter with the premise of this entire book – it is all about love, because as I was writing down everything I saw in the Word, I realized that our whole life we have had wrong thinking about money. To understand what you are about to read, you must turn to the Lord so that the veil can be removed. You must let the Spirit change your thoughts and attitudes so that you can take off your old nature that is corrupted by lust and deception and put on your new nature that is created to be like God, truly righteous and holy. Everything is about love, and the same is true for money. It is not about what we get, it has always been about what we give. We just didn't know it.

MONEY IS NOT THE BLESSING

First, we must understand that money is not the blessing. Then Jesus turned to His disciples and said,

> "God blesses you who are poor,
> for the Kingdom of God is yours.
> God blesses you who are hungry now,
> for you will be satisfied.
> God blesses you who weep now,
> for in due time you will laugh."

"What blessings await you when people hate you and exclude you and mock you and curse you as evil because you follow the Son of Man. When that happens, be happy! Yes, leap for joy! For a great reward awaits you in heaven. And remember, their ancestors treated the ancient prophets that same way." (Luke 6:20-23).

This does not even make sense to our natural way of thinking. God's blessings fall on those who are poor, hungry, and those who weep? He blesses those who are hated, excluded, and mocked? Then He goes on to say...

> "What sorrow awaits you who are rich,
> for you have your only happiness now.
> What sorrow awaits you who are fat and prosperous now,
> for a time of awful hunger awaits you.
> What sorrow awaits you who laugh now,
> for your laughing will turn to mourning and sorrow.
> What sorrow awaits you who are praised by the crowds,
> for their ancestors also praised false prophets."
> (Luke 6:24-26).

Now look at this list. Sorrow awaits those who are rich, fat and prosperous. Sorrow awaits those who laugh and are praised by the crowds. This is everything we are looking for in this life. We want to be rich and prosperous – maybe not fat. But we want to laugh and be praised by others. We don't want to be poor and hungry. We don't want to weep or be hated, excluded, and mocked.

Sweet Jesus, please let the Spirit change our thoughts and attitudes. We have had such wrong thinking. We thought that people who are rich were the ones who were blessed, but that is not so.

"Believers who are poor have something to boast about, for God has honored them. And those who are rich should boast that God has humbled them. They will fade away like a little flower in the field. The hot sun rises and the grass withers; the little flower droops and falls, and its beauty fades away. In the same way, the rich will fade away with all of their achievements." (James 1:9-11).

"So this is the situation: Most of the people of Israel have not found the favor of God they are looking for so earnestly. A few have – the ones God has chosen – but the hearts of the rest were hardened. As the Scriptures say,

> 'God has put them into a deep sleep.
> To this day He has shut their eyes so they do not see,
>   And closed their ears so they do not hear.'

> Likewise, David said,

> 'Let their bountiful table become a snare,
>   a trap that makes them think all is well.
> Let their blessings cause them to stumble,
>   and let them get what they deserve.
> Let their eyes go blind so they cannot see,
>   and let their backs be bent forever.'
> (Romans 11:7-10).

Our money has become a trap. We think everything is okay because we have money. It is not okay.

"Look here, you rich people: Weep and groan with anguish because of all the terrible troubles ahead of you. Your wealth is rotting away, and your fine clothes are moth-eaten rags. Your gold and silver are corroded. The very wealth you were counting on will eat away your flesh like fire. This corroded treasure you have hoarded will testify against you on the day of judgment. For listen! Hear the cries of the field workers whom you have cheated of their pay. The cries of those who harvest your fields have reached the ears of the LORD of Heaven's Armies."

"You have spent your years on earth in luxury, satisfying your every desire. You have fattened yourselves for the day of slaughter. You have condemned and killed innocent people, who do not resist you." (James 5:1-6).

Why am I giving these scriptures first when I want to talk about money? We live in America. We are rich. I want you to see what God thinks about money. God wants people to do what is right, but we end up doing a lot of things to get money that we should never do. It is a trap. Then what we do with the money is a trap. We must escape the trap. Money is not the blessing. Instead, money should always be used to bless.

So, what does God want us to do with money?

TITHE

"I am the LORD, and I do not change. That is why you descendants of Jacob are not already destroyed. Ever since the days of your ancestors, you have scorned My decrees and failed to obey them. Now return to Me, and I will return to you," says the LORD of Heaven's Armies.

> "But you say, 'How can we return when we have never gone away?'"
> "Should people cheat God? Yet you have cheated Me!"
> "But you ask, 'What do you mean? When did we ever cheat You?'"

"You have cheated Me of the tithes and offerings due to Me. You are under a curse, for your whole nation has been cheating Me. Bring all the tithes into the storehouse so there will be enough food in My Temple. If you do," says the LORD of Heaven's Armies, "I will open the windows of heaven for you. I will pour out a blessing so great you won't have enough room to take it in! Try it! Put Me to the test! Your crops will be abundant, for I will guard them from insects and disease. Your grapes will not fall from the vine before they are ripe," says the LORD of Heaven's Armies. Then all nations will call you blessed, for your land will be such a delight, "says the LORD of Heaven's Armies. (Malachi 3:6-12).

To tithe means to give the first ten percent of whatever we make to the local church. This money does not go to a charity or to a TV evangelist. It goes to the local church. This provides for the needs of the local body. This is so important to God because when we do this small thing, it shows God that we trust Him. When we give Him the first of everything we make or have, it shows God how important He is. This simple act of obedience will do two things. First, it helps get rid of the "love of money." It takes money off the throne of our heart so that God can then take His rightful place. Second, it allows God to work on our behalf.

There is a very real "devourer" that is loosed on the earth. He has permission to take or destroy everything we have if we are not tithing. We are under a financial curse. To stop this devourer, we tithe. God does the rest. He says, "Test Me in this! I will open up the windows of heaven and pour out a blessing on you that you will not be able to take it in." If we do not get this right, we will not make it in the coming days. God will not be our God, money will.

Once we commit to tithing, we are then in a position to give offerings. An offering is anything we give that will bless others. An offering can go to any person or place where God directs.

DON'T STORE UP TREASURES ON EARTH

"Don't store up treasures here on earth, where moths eat them and rust destroys them, and where thieves break in and steal. Store your treasures in heaven, where moths and rust cannot destroy, and thieves do not break in and steal. Wherever your treasure is, there the desires of your heart will also be." (Matthew 6:19-21).

You and I both know that there is no safe investment right now. Trillions of dollars disappear overnight. No one knows how or why. Poof. It is gone. However, there is one place we can put our money where it will always be safe – give to the poor, to those in need. This is how we lay up treasures in heaven. We help others.

"Oh, the joys of those who are kind to the poor! The LORD rescues them when they are in trouble. The LORD protects them and keeps them alive. He gives them prosperity in the land and rescues them from their enemies. The LORD nurses them when they are sick and restores them to health." (Psalm 41:1-3).

When we lay up treasures in heaven by giving to the poor, it opens the door for God to do such kind things for us. But more than that, wherever our treasure is, there our heart will be also. God is after our heart. He has our heart if we want to care for the poor.

Then the Lord said to him, "You Pharisees are so careful to clean the outside of the cup and the dish, but inside you are filthy – full of greed and wickedness! Fools! Didn't God make the inside as well as the outside? So clean the inside by giving gifts to the poor, and you will be clean all over." (Luke 11:39-41).

Wow! Did you hear that? If we give gifts to the poor, God will heal us of our greed and wickedness. The inside will be clean. This is amazing, and all we must do to be clean is give gifts to the poor.

Then Jesus told a rich man, "If you want to be perfect, go and sell all your possessions and give the money to the poor, and you will have treasure in heaven. Then come, follow Me." But when the young man heard this, he went away sad, for he had many possessions. (Matthew 19:21-22). To be perfect God just said, "Sell all you have and give to the poor." What? Money is not important to God, the poor are. This man could not do it, money was too important. He went away sorrowful. When Mark recorded this story, he said, "Looking at the man, Jesus felt genuine love for him." (Mark 10:21).

Jesus looked around and said to his disciples, "How hard it is for the rich to enter the Kingdom of God!" This amazed them. But Jesus said again, "Dear children, it is very hard to enter the Kingdom of God. In fact, it is easier for a camel to go through the eye of a needle than for a rich person to enter the Kingdom of God!"

The disciples were astounded. "Then who in the world can be saved?" they asked.

Jesus looked at them intently and said, "Humanly speaking, it is impossible. But not with God. Everything is possible with God."

Then Peter began to speak up. "We've given up everything to follow you," he said.

"Yes," Jesus replied, "and I assure you that everyone who has given up house or brothers or sisters or mother or father or children or property, for My sake and for the Good News, will receive now in return a hundred times as many houses, brothers, sisters, mothers, children, and property – along with persecution. And in the world to come that person will have eternal life. But many who are the greatest now will be least important then, and those who seem least important now will be the greatest then." (Mark 10:23-31).

We cannot outgive God. It is not possible. No matter what we have to give up, He multiplies it back to us on this earth and then in the world to come. Those who give much get much, and they will be considered the greatest in the Kingdom of Heaven.

DON'T LOOK AT MONEY

"Your eye is like a lamp that provides light for your body. When your eye is healthy, your whole body is filled with light. But when your eye is unhealthy, your whole body is filled with darkness. And if the light you think you have is actually darkness, how deep that darkness it! No one can serve two masters. For you will hate one and love the other; you will be devoted to one and despise the other. You cannot serve God and be enslaved to money." (Matthew 6:22-24).

What are we looking at? If we are looking at money, we are in darkness and we don't know where we are going. Don't make decisions based on money. It doesn't work. Look at Jesus, then you will be filled with light. You will know the right choice to make. Money will not be the factor. But what if we think we are looking at God, but we are really looking at money. How deep is that darkness. We cannot serve both God and money. They are leading us in opposite directions.

When I first got hold of this verse, I turned my back on money. I did not look at it. I did not think about it. I did not scheme about what to do with it. It became unimportant.

DON'T WORRY

"That is why I tell you not to worry about everyday life – whether you have enough food and drink, or enough clothes to wear. Isn't life more than food, and your body more than clothing? Look at the birds. They don't plant or harvest or store food in barns, for your heavenly Father feeds them. And aren't you far more valuable to Him than they are? Can all your worries add a single moment to your life?"

"And why worry about your clothing? Look at the lilies of the field and how they grow. They don't work or make their clothing, yet Solomon in all his glory was not dressed as beautifully as they are. And if God cares so wonderfully for wildflowers that are here today and thrown into the fire tomorrow, He will certainly care for you. Why do you have so little faith?"

"So don't worry about these things, saying, 'What will we eat? What will we drink? What will we wear? These things dominate the thoughts of unbelievers, but your heavenly Father already knows all your needs. Seek the Kingdom of God above all else, and live righteously, and He will give you everything you need. So don't worry about tomorrow, for tomorrow will bring its own worries. Today's trouble is enough for today." (Matthew 6:25-34).

Probably the thing people worry about the most is money. If worry is in your heart, face Jesus and tell Him, "I am guilty of worrying, will You forgive me?" Worry will then go away. Then turn your back on it and turn your face toward Jesus. Seek His face.

"Don't worry about anything; instead, pray about everything. Tell God what you need and thank Him for all He has done. Then you will experience God's peace, which exceeds anything we can understand. His peace will guard your hearts and minds as you live in Christ Jesus." (Philippians 4:6-7). If you do this, God's peace will protect you.

GIVE

"It would be good for you to finish what you started a year ago. Last year you were the first who wanted to give, and you were the first to begin doing it. Now you should finish what you started. Let the eagerness you showed in the beginning be matched now by your giving. Give in proportion to what you have. Whatever you give is acceptable if you give it eagerly. And give according to what you have, not what you don't have. Of course, I don't mean your giving should make life easy for others and hard for yourselves. I only mean that there should be some equality. Right now you have plenty and can to help those who are in need. Later they will have plenty and can share with you when you need it. In this way, things will be equal. As the Scriptures say,

> "Those who gathered a lot had nothing left over,
>   and those who gathered only a little had enough."
>   (2 Corinthians 8:10-15).

In the coming days we will all work together to make it. Pay attention to the needs of others. Sometimes our heart wants to do something, but we put it off and it never gets done. If you want to give, give.

GIVE GENEROUSLY

"Remember this – a farmer who plants only a few seeds will get a small crop. But the one who plants generously will get a generous crop. You must each decide in your heart how much to give. And don't give reluctantly or in response to pressure. 'For God loves a person who gives cheerfully. And God will generously provide all you need. Then you will always have everything you need and plenty left over to share with others. As the Scriptures say,

> "They share freely and give generously to the poor.
>   Their good deeds will be remembered forever."

"For God is the one who provides seed for the farmer and then bread to eat. In the same way, He will provide and increase your resources and then produce a great harvest of generosity in you."

"Yes, you will be enriched in every way so that you can always be generous. And when we take your gifts to those who need them, they will thank God. So two good things will result from this ministry of giving – the needs of the believers in Jerusalem will be met, and they will joyfully express their thanks to God."

"As a result of your ministry, they will give glory to God. For your generosity to them and to all believers will prove that you are obedient to the Good News of Christ. And they will pray for you with deep affection because of the overflowing grace God has given to you. Thank God for this gift too wonderful for words!" (2 Corinthians 9:6-15).

Our generosity to all believers proves that we are obedient to the Good News of Christ. This is God's plan. We join Him in taking care of the needs of others. It is God who provides seed for the farmer and bread to eat. He will provide and increase our resources and then provide a great harvest of generosity in us. We will be enriched in every way so that we can always be generous.

Wow! God does it all. Give and it shall be given to you. As we give to others, God gives more to us. Then we give more to others. We are all in this together. We will give generously to the poor. As a result of this ministry, God will get all the glory and people will pray for us with deep affection. What a plan!

This is what money is for. It is to give away. We have spent our life hoarding it, but no more. In the coming days we will see the very real needs of people, and we will act. We will be obedient to the Good News of Christ and these good deeds will be remembered forever.

LET GO

In America we all have so much stuff, and we want more stuff. But God says, "Do not love this world nor the things it offers you, for when you love the world, you do not have the love of the Father in you. For the world offers only a craving for the physical pleasure, a craving for everything we see, and pride in our achievements and possessions. These are not from the Father but are from this world. And this world is fading away, along with everything that people crave. But anyone who does what pleases God will live forever." (1 John 2:15-17).

Stuff moves us. We want it. We want others to see us have it. It is all pride and greed and covetousness and lust. These things will lead us into bondage. So what do we do? Let go. Turn to Jesus, open your heart wide and be honest. If you want what others have, tell Him. If there is pride in your heart, confess it as a sin and turn your back on it. If God reveals that there is greed in your heart, confess that, too. Let go of what you have. Don't let things move you. Does this seem too hard? It is. Turn your heart away from things and turn your face toward God. Let Him remove the veil. Let Him give you freedom.

BE CONTENT

"How I praise the Lord that you are concerned about me again. I know you have always been concerned for me, but you didn't have the chance to help me. Not that I was ever in need, for I have learned how to be content with whatever I have. I know how to live on almost nothing or with everything. I have learned the secret of living in every situation, whether it is with a full stomach or empty, with plenty or little. For I can do everything through Christ who gives me strength." (Philippians 4:10-14).

"True godliness with contentment is itself great wealth. After all, we brought nothing with us when we came into the world, and we can't take anything with us when we leave it. So if we have enough food and clothing, let us be content. But people who long to be rich fall into temptation and are trapped by many foolish and harmful desires that plunge them into ruin and destruction. For the love of money is the root of all kinds of evil. And some people, craving money, have wandered from the true faith and pierced themselves with many sorrows." (1 Timothy 6:6-10).

In America we want bigger, better things. When is enough, enough? Let it be enough. Be content.

Take a moment to sit at the feet of Jesus. Open your heart wide. Be real. Be honest. Talk to Him and let Him talk to you. Let Him tell you what He wants you to do with your money. Listen. Obey.

GIVE THANKS

"Always be joyful. Never stop praying. Be thankful in all circumstances, for this is God's will for you who belong to Christ." (1 Thessalonians 5:16-18). No matter what happens, rejoice and give thanks. We have no idea what honor this brings to God or how many doors in the heavens it opens for us.

In the coming days things are going to get hard financially. Don't quench the spirit by mummering and complaining. Instead, fix your eyes on Jesus, guard your heart, and give thanks. God is ALWAYS up to something good.

10. HOW TO FIND GOD'S FAVOR IN OUR RELATIONSHIPS.

Since God's favor means that we will all walk in perfect love, we have to understand how to get there. We must start by letting God heal us.

We all live in a very broken world. Nearly all of us have been lied to, abused, neglected, rejected, tossed aside, and abandoned in some area of our life. There is distrust and anger and bitterness and sorrow and pain that rule in our hearts. Many have built up walls and boarded up windows and locked doors. No one can get in, not even God. We have done things that we should never have done, and we have had things done to us that should never have been done, so we hide.

But now God is standing at the door knocking. He is the healer. He is the deliverer, and He is coming to rescue us. All we have to do is let Him. Before we can begin to walk in the favor of God, we must let Him heal us. But how?

OPEN YOUR HEART WIDE TO JESUS

Right now, face Jesus and open your heart wide. Let Him hold you. Let Him wrap His unfailing love around you. Let Him speak comforting words over you. Rest. Rest in His arms for a while.

Then speak to Him. Be honest. If you are angry, tell Him. If you are disappointed, let Him know. Then let Him into every broken, dark, painfilled, rejected area of your heart. Let Him shine the light of His love. Don't hold anything back. Let Him see it all. He knows it anyway. Then let go. Tell Him you don't want it anymore. Say, "I am sorry for holding onto the pain and the sorrow of the past. Please forgive me. Set me free. I am sorry for holding onto the anger and bitterness and unforgiveness. I don't want to live like this any longer." One by one, give Him your hurt and your pain. Then ask Him to fill you with His unfailing love.

FORGIVE

To be truly free, we must forgive the person or people who hurt us. We must come to God without excuse and say, "I am guilty of holding onto unforgiveness, will You forgive me?" And He will. Your heart will feel immediately lighter. But then according to God's Word which says, "Love those who hate you, bless those who curse you, and pray for those who spitefully use you," begin to pray for those who hurt you.

"LORD, please don't hold their sins against them. Heal their broken hearts. Set them free. Send light and truth. Send mercy and grace. Send Your unfailing love and send Your kindness that leads to repentance. Forgive generously, LORD. May Your greatest blessings be theirs. I am asking this in the mighty name of Jesus. AMEN." This prayer may or may not change them, but it will change you. Pray for them always.

FORGIVE YOURSELF

For some people the most important person you must forgive is yourself. Some people cannot let go of the regret and shame and guilt and sorrow of the sins of the past. But we must know that everyone has sinned. We are all in this together. "If we claim we have no sin, we are only fooling ourselves and not living in the truth. But if we confess our sins to Him, He is faithful and just to forgive us our sins and to cleanse us from all wickedness. If we claim we have not sinned, we are calling God a liar and showing that His word has no place in our hearts." (1 John 1:8-10).

All of us are sinners. Keep that in mind. There is no one righteous, no not one. But one of the greatest promises we have in the Word of God is that if we confess our sins, He is faithful and just to forgive us our sins and to cleanse us from all wickedness. Wow! It works. Do it. Turn to Jesus and start confessing all that you have done that you are not proud of. Don't leave anything out. He already knows everything we have done - every thought that we think, every word we have spoken, and every meditation of our heart. He knows it all. Confess it, and it goes away! It is amazing.

But sometimes the regret and shame and guilt and sorrow of the past refuse to leave. If we confess these as sins, too, they go away. Try it. Say, "God, I have held onto guilt and shame and sorrow and regret for so long. I don't want it anymore. Will you take it away!" And He does. Peace enters. It is so amazing.

But there are also other enemies that attack God's people: self-condemnation, feelings of worthlessness, thinking we are not good enough, feelings of failure and inadequacy. These are all lies, and they are bullies. AND they live inside of us. Kick them out. Say, "God, please forgive me for condemning myself. I am guilty and I am sorry. Forgive me for believing a lie that I am not good enough, that I am worthless and inadequate and a failure. You said that I am Your workmanship created in Christ Jesus for good works that You prepared in advance that I should walk in. I want to walk in those good works, and I can't do it until you heal me and set me free. You said that I am fearfully and wonderfully made in Your image. Teach me to believe and trust this truth. I ask this in Jesus' name. Amen."

If you have prayed these prayers, your heart should feel relief. Your enemies have been kicked out. Now, ask God to replace those spirits with His unfailing love. "LORD, I open my heart wide to receive Your goodness. Fill me with Your love and joy and peace and patience and kindness and goodness and gentleness and faithfulness and self-control. Fill my heart with mercy and grace and compassion. Send Your light and Your truth. Let them lead me to Your holy hill and to Your tabernacle. Be kind to me, LORD, and let this kindness lead me to repentance. I am asking this in the mighty name of Jesus. Amen."

Be kind to yourself. Give yourself mercy and grace. Rest in God's forgiveness.

FORGIVE GOD

For most people life has not turned out as they would have hoped. We are disappointed. Sometimes we get mad, and we start to blame God. We point our finger at Him because we know He could have changed the outcome.

What we don't understand is that God has His own plans. These are good plans, plans to prosper and not to harm, plans to give us hope and a future. These plans are eternal. We are looking at everything that is temporary, but God uses these temporary things to turn our hearts toward what is forever.

"Even before He made the world, God loved us and chose us in Christ to be holy and without fault in His eyes. God decided in advance to adopt us into His own family by bringing us to Himself through Jesus Christ. This is what He wanted to do, and it gave Him great pleasure. So we praise God for the glorious grace He has poured out on us who belong to His dear Son. He is so rich in kindness and grace that He purchased our freedom with the blood of His Son and forgave our sins. He has showered His kindness on us, along with all wisdom and understanding."

"God has now revealed to us His mysterious will regarding Christ – which is to fulfill HIS OWN GOOD PLAN. And this is the plan: At the right time He will bring everything together under the authority of Christ – everything in heaven and on earth. Furthermore, because we are united with Christ, we have received an inheritance from God, for He chose us in advance, and He makes everything work out according to His plan." (Ephesians 1:4-11).

When we finally turn our hearts to see things from God's perspective, we can begin to understand. God's plan is that we will all be holy and without fault, blameless before Him. The only way He can do that is through the blood of His Son. When we are "in Christ," – trusting Him fully, God will bring all things together under the authority of Christ – everything in heaven (the things that are eternal) and on earth (the things that are temporary). God then showers His kindness on us along with all wisdom and understanding. God's plan is so much better than our plan.

God makes everything work out according to His plan. He guides the footsteps of the godly, and He delights in every detail of their lives. Though they stumble, they will never fall, for He holds them in His right hand.

Trust it. God's plan is better. He knows what He is doing, we don't. So, if there is any anger and blame in your heart toward God, go to Him. Tell Him. He already knows. Tell Him you are sorry, and then ask Him to fill your heart with wisdom and understanding. Ask Him to teach you to trust His plan. He will.

STOP JUDGING OTHERS

If we truly understood how wicked it is to judge others, we would never do it. To put one person above or beneath anyone else is not God's way. There is no one who is better than anyone else. We are all fearfully and wonderfully made in the image of God, and we are all horribly wicked sinners. We are all in this together.

Romans 1 talks about the wickedness of man. "But God shows His anger from heaven against all sinful, wicked people who suppress the truth by their wickedness. They know the truth about God because He has made it obvious to them. For ever since the world was created, people have seen the earth and sky. Through everything God made, they can clearly see His invisible qualities – His eternal power and divine nature. So they have no excuse for not knowing God." (Romans 1:18-20).

None of us has an excuse for not knowing God. Creation declares that there is a Creator. "Yes, they knew God, but they wouldn't worship Him as God or even give Him thanks. And they began to think up foolish ideas of what God was like. As a result, their minds became dark and confused. Claiming to be wise, they instead became utter fools. And instead of worshiping the glorious, ever-living God, they worshiped idols made to look like mere people and birds and animals and reptiles."

"So God abandoned then to do whatever shameful things their hearts desired. As a result, they did vile and degrading things with each other's bodies. They traded the truth about God for a lie. So they worshiped and served the things God created instead of the Creator Himself, who is worthy of eternal praise! Amen. That is why God abandoned them to their shameful desires. Even the women turned against the natural way to have sex and instead indulged in sex with each other. And the men, instead of having normal sexual relations with women, burned with lust for each other. Men did shameful things with other men, and as a result of this sin, they suffered within themselves the penalty they deserved."

"Since they thought it foolish to acknowledge God, He abandoned them to their foolish thinking and let them do things that should never be done. Their lives became full of every kind of wickedness, sin, greed, hate, envy, murder, quarreling, deception, malicious behavior, and gossip. They are backstabbers, haters of God, insolent, proud, and boastful. They invent new ways of sinning, and they disobey their parents. They refuse to understand, break their promises, are heartless, and have no mercy. They know God's justice requires that those who do these things deserve to die, yet they do them anyway. Worse yet, they encourage others to do them, too." (Romans 1:21-32).

This is the result of worshiping and serving the creation rather than the Creator. This is the wickedness of mankind. We can see it. But Romans 2 goes on to say:

"You may think you can condemn such people, but you are just as bad, and you have no excuse! When you say they are wicked and should be punished, you are condemning yourself, for you who judge others do these very same things. Since you judge others for doing these things, how do you think you can avoid God's judgment when you do the same things? Don't you see how wonderfully kind, tolerant, and patient God is with you? Does this mean nothing to you? Can't you see that His kindness is intended to turn you from your sin?" (Romans 2:1-4).

God spends most of chapter one in Romans telling about the sinful nature of mankind, but in chapter two, He doesn't talk about the sin of the world, but the sin of judgment. When we judge others, we condemn ourselves. That is crazy, but that is what it says. If we continue to judge others, we will not escape the judgment of God.

"Do not judge others, and you will not be judged. For you will be treated as you treat others. The standard you use in judging is the standard by which you will be judged." (Matthew 7:1-2). If we don't judge others, we will not be judged, but if we continue to judge others, we will be judged by the same standard we use to judge others. The cup of judgment that is in our own hand will be the cup used to pour judgment onto us, and the judgment of God is not fun.

"And why worry about a speck in your friend's eye when you have a log in your own? How can you think of saying to your friend, 'Let me help you get rid of that speck in your eye,' when you can't see past the log in your own eye? Hypocrite! First get rid of the log in your own eye; then you will see well enough to deal with the speck in your friend's eye." (Matthew 7:3-5).

God describes sin as a speck and judgment as a log. The judgment that is in us is far worse than the sin that is in the world. We must get judgment out of our heart!

When God started delivering me from judgment, it came in five parts. I want to share with you what God taught me.

STOP JUDGING THE CHURCH

First, He said, "Stop judging the church!" "Who are you to condemn someone else's servants? Their own master will judge whether they stand or fall. And with the Lord's help, they will stand and receive His approval." (Romans 14:4). We must stop judging the people of the church, and we must stop judging the churches themselves. Instead, let us pray for one another. "I urge you, first of all, to pray for all people. Ask God to help them; intercede on their behalf, and give thanks for them." (1 Timothy 2:1).

Wow! Pray this way for all people, but especially those in the church. Thank God for them. Ask Him to help them and intercede for them. If they are off track, pray. Intercede. Ask God to help. Thank God for them. We are all in this together. Let's be on each other's side!

STOP JUDGING THE WORLD

Second, God said, "Stop judging the world." Go back and read the passage out of Romans 1. You can see how wicked we have become. We have turned our back on God, and sin is the result, but for God's people, we must stop judging the world. We must be for them and not against them. Except for the grace of God, that would be us. "I urge you, first of all, to PRAY FOR ALL PEOPLE. Ask God to help them;

intercede on their behalf, and GIVE THANKS FOR THEM. Pray this way for kings and all who are in authority so that we can live peaceful and quiet lives marked by godliness and dignity. This is good and pleases God our Savior, who WANTS EVERYONE TO BE SAVED AND TO UNDERSTAND THE TRUTH. For,

> 'There is one God and one Mediator who can reconcile God and humanity – the man Christ Jesus. He gave His life to purchase freedom FOR EVERYONE.'"

"This is the message God gave to the world at just the right time." (1 Timothy 2:1-6).

Our God wants everyone to be saved and to know the truth. Jesus gave His life to purchase freedom for everyone. Don't take that lightly. Every person is a person for whom Jesus died. Each person is supremely important to God, so they must become supremely important to us, too. We must stop judging the world.

WHY ARE YOU TELLING HIM WHAT HE SHOULD DO IN YOUR HEART?

Then God asked me, "Why are you telling him what he should do in your heart?" Several years ago, my youngest son had back problems. He had to stay flat on his back for six weeks so that he could be approved to do surgery. During that time my daughter-in-law had two small children, a stressful job, and a husband she had to take care of. When Valentine's Day was getting close, I suggested to my son that he do something kind for his wife. He agreed. As the time got closer, I suggested it again, but this time he resisted. He did not want to be told what to do.

As I worked in the shop, grumbling in my heart, the LORD spoke to me. "Why are you telling him what he should do in your heart? Did it ever occur to you that I am telling him what he should do in his heart?"

"What, God? Stubborn rebellion, and You are telling him what he should do in his heart?" The LORD said, "Yes." Wow. We have no clue.

I told God, "Please forgive me for telling my son what he should do in my heart." Then I went to my son and said, "Will you forgive me for telling you what you should do in my heart?" He had no clue what I was talking about, but that day my attitude toward my son changed. I no longer saw what he didn't do, I saw the amazing man he was. This was a game changer. Now I speak the truth and love people. I let them make their own choices because no one is going to change their heart except God. I rest in the fact that God is in control, and He is good. He has good plans for my family, plans to prosper and not to harm, plans to give hope and a future. And I TRY to stay out of God's way.

SHE IS ADEQUATE, AND SO ARE YOU.

Several years ago, God taught me that we are all good enough for the job God has set before us. I live in Texas, and in Texas, theatre competition is a big deal. I happen to judge some of the One Act Play contests in this area. These contests are now paneled, so there are three judges for each contest. Each judge gives his/her opinion and critique of each play.

One year, after the first competition, I went into the shop and all these thoughts were going on in my head. "You should have said this." "Why didn't you say that?" "They are going to think." Because I had lived in peace for several years, I turned to God and asked, "What is going on?"

He then allowed me to remember that a thought had crossed my mind that one of the judges was not a very good judge. I never said it. I didn't dwell on it, I just thought it. Then God said, "She is adequate, and so are you." Oh my goodness! The relief. She is good enough for what God is asking her to do, and so am I. If someone is assigned a job, they are going to be equipped to do the job. It might not be how you would do it. It might not be as amazing as someone else might do, but it is adequate. Honor it. Honor the person doing it. She is enough and so are you.

FRESH WATER AND BITTER WATER SHOULD NOT COME FROM THE SAME FOUNTAIN.

The final? message God gave me about judgment was found in James. "People can tame all kinds of animals, birds, reptiles, and fish, but no one can tame the tongue. It is restless and evil, full of deadly poison. Sometimes it praises our Lord and Father, and sometimes it curses those who have been made in the image of God. And so blessing and cursing come pouring out of the same mouth. Surely, my brothers and sisters, this is not right! Does a spring of water bubble out with both fresh water and bitter water? Does a fig tree produce olives, or a grapevine produce figs? No, and you can't draw fresh water from a salty spring." (James 3:7-12).

When I saw this, God said, "Who is not made in My image? Hitler was made in My image. You cannot bless God and curse man – any man." Oh, my goodness! I am so sorry, God. I now refuse to speak anything but blessings over every person I meet. I want my well to be fresh water. We have no idea what we are saying and what we are doing. We must let the Spirit change our thoughts and attitudes. We must take off the old and put on the new. We must learn to know our Creator and become like Him -- truly righteous and holy. God loves people. God wants us to love people, too.

To walk in the favor of God, we must get judgment out of our heart.

HONOR OTHERS

If we are going to walk in perfect love, we must learn to honor people. All people. To honor a person means to hold him up in respect and high esteem. Man was created to be honored. "What are mere mortals that you should think about them, or a son of man that you should care for him? Yet for a little while You made them a little lower than the angels and crowned them with glory and honor. You gave them authority over all things." (Hebrews 2:6-8).

We were created for honor, but we live in a time period where honor has been stripped. No matter what we do or how hard we try, we are being knocked down. We don't know how to honor one another. We don't even know how to show respect. But God's kingdom is a kingdom of honor, and it is a kingdom of respect. To fit into this kingdom, we must learn how to honor and respect people.

CHILDREN HONOR YOUR PARENTS

"Children, obey your parents because you belong to the Lord, for this is the right thing to do. Honor your father and mother. This is the first commandment with a promise: If you honor your father and mother, things will go well for you, and you will have a long life on the earth." (Ephesians 6:1-3).

Honor starts in the home. It starts when we are children, and it starts with obedience. To obey our parents is to show that we honor them. To obey without complaining is great honor. So we must start by doing what our parents ask us to do.

But what about those parents who are not good parents?   There are many children who have been physically, mentally, sexually, or verbally abused. The commandment did not say to honor only the fathers and mothers who are good, it says, "Honor your father and mother." But the scars are real. If this is the case, you must let God heal your heart and set you free in order to do what the Lord is asking you to do. Go to the first of this chapter and work your way through it. Let God heal you. Forgive. Let go. Then pray for your parents. Be on their side. Then ask God what honor looks like and do it. Lift them high in your heart. Speak encouraging, affirming words to them. Tell them how important they are. Serve them. Be on their side. This includes adult parents.

Remember, the time of God's favor has come. He will help us do this. "Look, I am sending you the prophet Elijah before the great and dreadful Day of the LORD arrives. His preaching will turn the hearts of fathers to their children, and the hearts of children to their fathers. Otherwise, I will come and strike the land with a curse." (Malachi 3:5-6). If we don't turn and start to honor our parents, our land will be struck with a curse.

WIVES HONOR YOUR HUSBANDS

Wives, honor your husbands. Peter talks about this when he talks about slaves in in 1 Peter 2, then in 1 Peter 3, he said, "In the same way, you wives must accept the authority of your husbands." So I am going to start in 1 Peter 2 to talk to wives. I will insert wives and husbands instead of slaves and masters.

"You who are wives must submit to your husbands with all respect. Do what they tell you – not only if they are kind and reasonable, but even if they are cruel. For God is pleased when, conscious of His will, you patiently endure unjust treatment. Of course, you get no credit for being patient if you are beaten for doing wrong. But if you suffer for doing good and endure it patiently, God is pleased with you. For God called you to do good, even if it means suffering, just as Christ suffered for you." (1 Peter 2:18-20).

Are you listening to this? God is pleased when we suffer for doing good and endure it patiently. We are called to honor and respect our husbands no matter what they do. That means to be on his side. Pray for him. Thank God for him. Ask God to help him. Never speak evil of him. Never let your thoughts think evil of him.

"Christ is your example, and you must follow in His steps.

> He never sinned,
> Nor ever deceived anyone.
> He did not retaliate when He was insulted,
> Nor threaten revenge when He suffered.
> He left His case in the hands of God,
> Who always judges fairly.
> He personally carried our sins
> In His body on the cross
> So that we can be dead to sin
> And live for what is right.
> By His wounds
> You are healed.
> Once you were like sheep
> Who wandered away.
> But now you have turned to your Shepherd,
> The Guardian of your souls. "(1 Peter 2:21-25).

Turn to your Shepherd, the Guardian of your soul when things get tough. Let Him heal you. Let Him set you free. Let Him teach you how to do it right.

"In the same way, you wives must accept the authority of your husbands. Then, even if some refuse to obey the Good News, your godly lives will speak to them without any words. They will be won over by observing your pure and reverent lives." (1 Peter 3:1-2). If we can learn to treat our husbands with honor and respect, our actions will speak louder than any words ever could. Even if your husband is not a

Christian, God can use your godly life to preach to him. Every man needs to be respected and honored. For a man to be honored by his wife is the greatest honor of all. We must not withhold that honor from him.

"Don't be concerned about the outward beauty of fancy hairstyles, expensive jewelry, or beautiful clothes. You should clothe yourselves instead with the beauty that comes from within, the unfading beauty of a gentle and quiet spirit, which is so precious to God. This is how the holy women of old made themselves beautiful. They put their trust in God and accepted the authority of their husbands. For instance, Sarah obeyed her husband, Abraham, and called him her master. You are her daughters when you do what is right without fear of what your husbands might do." (1 Peter 3:3-6).

If you want to be beautiful, ladies, put your trust in God and accept the authority of your husband. Do what is right. Don't be afraid of what he might do. Be gentle and kind and obedient and honoring. Trust God to do the rest.

HUSBANDS HONOR YOUR WIVES

"In the same way, you husbands must give honor to your wives. Treat your wife with understanding as you live together. She may be weaker than you are, but she is your equal partner in God's gift of new life. Treat her as you should so your prayers will not be hindered."
(1 Peter 3:7).

IN THE SAME WAY, husbands honor your wives. Lift her up in high esteem and high respect. Try to understand her. Encourage her. Validate her. Treat her right so your prayers will not be hindered.

"And further, submit to one another out of reverence for Christ. For husbands, this means love your wives, just as Christ loved the church. He gave up his life for her to make her holy and clean, washed by the cleansing of God's word. He did this to present her to Himself as a glorious church without a spot or wrinkle or any other blemish. Instead, she will be holy and without fault. In the same way, husbands ought to love their wives as they love their own bodies. For a man who loves his wife actually shows love for himself." (Ephesians 5:21, 25-28).

Submit to one another out of reverence for Christ. Listen to your wife. Hear what she has to say. Love her. Give your life for her. Present her to God. Wash her with the cleansing of God's word. Speak life over her. Protect her. Defend her. Provide for her. Honor her. Love her like you love yourself. To love your wife is actually showing love for yourself.

If we are going to learn how to honor people, we must start at home. Look at those who are closest to you. Ask God to show you what He wants you to do.

HONOR THOSE WHO ARE IN AUTHORITY

In America nearly every line of authority has been crossed. It is nearly impossible to lead. People will not let us. There is rebellion against every type of authority that would hold us accountable. But God's kingdom is a kingdom of authority. Each person submits to and honors the authority of those above him. When this happens, there is order. But as you can tell, there is no honor for authority in this country, so there is no order. So how do we fix it? We can't. All we can do is become obedient to what God is asking each of us to do.

"Everyone must submit to governing authorities. For all authority comes from God, and those in positions of authority have been placed there by God. So anyone who rebels against authority is rebelling against what God has instituted, and they will be punished." (Romans 13:1-2).

We must understand that all authority is put there by God. He chooses. It is God who chooses who gets into office, who gets the promotion, who becomes the next President. Even if it is by crooked means, it is still God who puts the people in charge. He puts them there for His own purposes. Each person who is in authority is there for a reason.

Nebuchadnezzar learned this lesson the hard way. One night he had a dream, and when Daniel came to interpret the dream, this is what he said.

"This is what the dream means, Your Majesty, and what the Most High has declared will happen to my lord the king. You will be driven from human society, and you will live in the fields with the wild animals. You will east grass like a cow, and you will be drenched with the dew of heaven. Seven periods of time will pass while you live this way, until you learn that the Most High rules over the kingdoms of the world and gives them to anyone He chooses." (Daniel 4:24-25). Twelve months later all these things happened to King Nebuchadnezzar until he learned that heaven rules. (Daniel 4:26).

So, we must realize that if there is anyone in any position in authority over us, he/she was put there by God. Our responsibility is to submit to those in authority. "They are God's servants, sent for the very purpose of punishing those who do what is wrong. So you must submit to them, not only to avoid punishment, but also to keep a clear conscience." (Romans 13:4-5). Those who are in authority are put there to punish those who do what is wrong. When we choose to rebel against authority, we are choosing to rebel against what God has instituted, and we will be punished.

We must understand that God chooses who is in authority, and they are put in this position to punish those who rebel. If we rebel against the authority, we are actually rebelling against God. That is a lot to take in considering that most of us do not think that those who are in authority in our country are honest and dependable men and women of integrity. Then Paul goes on to say, "Give to everyone what you owe them: Pay your taxes and government fees to those who collect them and GIVE RESPECT AND HONOR TO THOSE WHO ARE IN AUTHORITY." (Romans 13:7).

Oh, my goodness! How far we have fallen. Forgive us, LORD, for what we have done. Forgive us for what we think. Forgive us for what we have said. We are guilty of having rebellion in our heart, and according to Your Word, we deserve to be punished. You have sent those who are in authority over us to punish us. LORD, teach us how to do it right. Teach us how to honor and respect those who are over us, especially those who are trying to govern us. Send Your favor, LORD. We cannot do this without You. In Jesus' name. Amen.

There is a prayer in 1 Timothy 2:1-6 that will help us get to where we need to go. "I urge you, first of all, to pray for all people. Ask God to help them; intercede on their behalf and give thanks for them. Pray this way for KINGS AND ALL WHO ARE IN AUTHORITY so that we can live peaceful and quiet lives marked by godliness and dignity. This is good and pleases God our Savior, who wants everyone to be saved and to understand the truth. For,

> There is one God and one Mediator who can reconcile God and all humanity – the man Christ Jesus. He gave His life to purchase freedom for everyone.

This is the message God gave to the world at just the right time."

In order to live peaceful, quiet lives marked by godliness and dignity, we must pray for all people like this, especially our President and those who are in authority. It does not matter if the President comes from the right or the left, the command is the same. God wants everyone to be saved and to understand the truth. It does not matter if it is Kamala Harris or Donald Trump who gets to be President. Jesus gave His life to purchase freedom for them both. Our job is to pray for them, ask God to help them, give thanks for them, and intercede on their behalf. Our lives will then be quiet and peaceful. We will be filled with godliness and dignity. This is going to be supremely important in the coming days.

AMERICA IN REAL TIME

America is in a perilous place. It is a powder keg. We are a divided people filled with entitlement and hatred. Each party is pointing the finger at the other party spewing hate-filled, mocking, slanderous dialogue. We are burning our house down with our words. There is no honor, there is no respect, and a house divided can never stand.

I cannot see any good coming out of the upcoming election. I cannot see either party conceding to the other. If one party wins, the cry will be, "Fraud." If the other party wins, the cry will be, "Felon, liar." It is a no-win situation, and neither party will stand down. In my opinion, we are on the brink of a civil war. And in the middle of all the hatred and division, America is armed with an arsenal of guns and ammunition. Everyone is prepared. But what does God say?

I said, "Plant the good seeds of righteousness, and you will harvest a crop of love. Plow up the hard ground of your hearts, for now is the time to seek the LORD, that He may come and shower righteousness upon you." (Hosea 10:12).

Right now, God is asking us to make different choices than what we did in the past. He wants us to plant seeds of righteousness so that we can harvest love. Now. Not tomorrow. Now is the time to turn to God and trust Him.

"But you have cultivated wickedness and harvested a thriving crop of sins. You have eaten the fruit of lies – trusting in your military might, believing that great armies could make your nation safe. Now, the terrors of war will rise among your people. All your fortifications will fall." (Hosea 10:13-14).

If we continue to think that our guns will keep us safe in the coming days, we are eating the fruit of lies, and we are cultivating wickedness and we will harvest a thriving crop of sins. Instead of love, we will get wickedness and sin. The choice is ours. But you say, "This choice is too hard. I can't do it."

"O Israel," says the LORD, "If you wanted to return to Me you could. You could throw away your detestable idols and stray away no more. Then when you swear by My name, saying, 'As surely as the LORD lives,' you could do so with truth, justice, and righteousness. Then you would be a blessing to the nations of the world, and all people would come and praise My name."

This is what the LORD says to the people of Judah and Jerusalem: "Plow up the hard ground of your hearts! Do not waste your good seed among thorns (the world). O people of Judah and Jerusalem, surrender your pride and power. Change your hearts before the LORD, or My anger will burn like an unquenchable fire because of all your sins." (Jeremiah 4:1-4).

In order to make it in the coming days, we will all have to surrender our pride and our power. We will have to throw away our detestable idols. The choice is ours, and we can do it if we want to. God will make a way of escape. This is the time of the LORD's favor.

NEVER LET LOYALTY AND KINDNESS LEAVE YOU

"My child, never forget the things I have taught you. Store My commands in your heart. If you do this, you will live many years, and your life will be satisfying. Never let loyalty and kindness leave you! Tie them around your neck as a reminder. Write them deep within your heart. Then you will find favor with both God and people, and you will earn a good reputation." (Proverbs 3:1-4).

If we want to find the favor of God, as well as the favor or people, we must forever be loyal and kind. But loyal and kind to whom? To everyone. This is where we have really messed up. We thought that we could choose who we can be kind and loyal to, but we cannot. God wants us to be kind to all people. He wants us to be loyal. But what does that mean?

It means to always be on his side. Always have his back. Always defend him. Always protect him. Be sincere. Do whatever we can to keep him safe. This means even the people who are against us, even those who would like nothing better than to destroy us, even to kill us. Be kind. Be loyal. And you will find favor with God and man, and you will earn a good reputation.

Then right after this verse is says, "Trust in the LORD with all your heart; do not depend on your own understanding. Seek His will in all you do, and He will show you which path to take." (Proverbs 3:5-6). If we are going to be loyal and kind to everyone in the coming days, we are going to have to trust God. We cannot depend on what we understand because times are going to be tough, and people are going to be mean. But if we do this, God will guide us along every path we should take.

"Don't be impressed with your own wisdom. Instead, fear the LORD and turn away from evil. Then you will have healing for your body and strength for your bones." (Proverbs 3:7-8). Do we want healing for our body and strength for our bones? We must fear God and turn from evil. This includes being kind and loyal.

"Honor the LORD with your wealth and with the best part of everything you produce. Then He will fill your barns with grain, and your vats will overflow with good wine." (Proverbs 3:9-10). If we honor the LORD with all of the good things we have, being kind to people, He will make sure that are barns are full and that we have plenty to eat and to give away.

"My child, don't reject the LORD's discipline, and don't be upset when He corrects you. For the LORD corrects those He loves, just as a father corrects a child in whom he delights." (Proverbs 3:11-12). I think in the coming days we are all going to be corrected. We have been going the wrong way, and God will not let us do that any longer. He loves us too much, and He delights over each of us. God is good to His people. Trust it.

CONCLUSION

As I am sitting here writing down everything the LORD is speaking to me, I can see that we have a long way to go. None of us are righteous, no not one. But, if we will keep turning to Jesus, He will do the rest. No matter what happens, turn to Jesus, and let Him remove the veil. Let Him heal us. Let Him set us free. Let Him teach us His ways and show us His paths. Then we will stop judging each other; instead, we will honor and be kind and loyal to all people – the good, the bad, and the ugly. ALL PEOPLE. Jesus lived for, loved, and died for all people. Let us live for, love, and die for them, too. This is a lot to ask, but it is true. God wants us to live like Jesus did on the earth.

"God is love, and all who live in love live in God, and God lives in them. And as we live in God, our love grows more perfect. So we will not be afraid on the Day of judgment, but we can face Him with confidence because we live like Jesus here in this world." (1 John 4:6-7). The Day of judgment is here, but if we live in love, we will not be afraid. We will face God with confidence because we live like Jesus. This is a very high calling, but if we keep turning to Jesus and live in Him, it is possible.

I want to leave this very long chapter with one final scripture. "Don't just pretend to love others. Really love them. Hate what is wrong. Hold tightly to what is good. Love each other with genuine (sincere) affection and take delight in honoring each other." (Romans 12:9-10). I am trying with everything in me to figure out how to live out this scripture. I want to really love people. I want to hate what is evil, but I want to cling to the good in each person. I want to be genuine and sincere, kind and loyal, and I want to delight in honoring them.

I think it is love and honor and respect and value that the whole world is seeking. They are looking for it in all the wrong places. They don't know that all of these are found in Jesus. My goal is to learn to love, honor, respect, and value all people so that they can see Jesus - the real Jesus. I want them to want Him as much as I do.

11. GOD IS LOOKING FOR CERTAIN RESPONSES FROM HIS CHILDREN.

There is a way of God that is right, and there is a path of God that takes us there. We just must find the right way and the right path. "Show me the right path, O LORD; point out the road for me to follow. Lead me by your truth and teach me, for You are the God who saves me. All day long I put my hope in You." (Psalm 25:4-5).

Our heart cry is to do what is right, but often we are not exactly sure what that is. Now the LORD is going to show us. Both Isaiah 2 and Micah 4 give us this promise.

"In the last days, the mountain of the LORD's house will be the highest of all – the most important place on earth. It will be raised above the other hills, and people from all over the world will stream there to worship. People from many nations will come and say, 'Come, let us go up to the mountain of the LORD, to the house of Jacob's God. THERE HE WILL TEACH US HIS WAYS, AND WE WILL WALK IN HIS PATHS.'

"For the LORD's teaching will go out from Zion; His word will go out from Jerusalem. And the LORD will mediate between peoples and will settle disputes between strong nations far away. They will hammer their swords into plowshares and their spears into pruning hooks. Nation will no longer fight against nation, nor train for war anymore. Everyone will live in peace and prosperity, enjoying their own grapevines and fig trees, for there will be nothing to fear. The LORD of Heaven's Armies has made this promise! Though the nations around us follow their idols, we will follow the LORD our God forever and ever."

"In that coming day," says the LORD, "I will gather together those who are lame, those who have been exiles, and those whom I have filled with grief. Those who are weak will survive as a remnant; those who were exiles will become a strong nation. Then I, the LORD, will rule from Jerusalem as their king forever." "As for you, Jerusalem, the citadel of God's people, your royal might and power will come back to you again. The kingship will be restored to My precious Jerusalem." (Micah 4:1-8).

God has made this promise that in the last days He would teach us His ways and show us His paths. No longer will we fight against each other. He will gather us together and restore our kingship and our might and power. He is going to do it all. It is a part of His big, good plan, but we must do our part, too. It is our job to listen to what He has to say and do it. When we choose to obey God's commands, we are showing God how much we love Him, and we are showing Him that we trust Him. We honor God when we obey Him. This is the response God is always looking for. He wants us to trust Him. Circumstances do not matter. Obedience does. So, what response is God wanting?

SUBMISSION and RESPECT

Submission is a nearly nonexistent concept in our country. Even if we submit for a moment, we nearly always find a way around it. And I don't see respect anywhere, but if we want God to teach us His ways and show us His paths, we must come to the place of submission and respect.

"For the Lord's sake, submit to ALL human authority – whether the king as head of state, or the officials he has appointed. For the king has sent them to punish those who do wrong and to honor those who do right."

"It is God's will that your honorable lives should silence those ignorant people who make foolish accusations against you. For you are free, yet you are God's slaves, so don't use your freedom as an excuse to do evil. Respect everyone and love the brotherhood. Fear God and respect the king."

"You who are slaves must submit to your masters with all respect. Do what they tell you – not only if they are kind and reasonable, but even if they are cruel. For God is pleased when, conscious of His will, you patiently endure unjust treatment. Of course, you get no credit for being patient if you are beaten for doing wrong. But if you suffer for doing good and endure it patiently, God is pleased with you. For God called you to do good, even if it means suffering, just as Christ suffered for you. He is your example, and you must follow in His steps." (1 Peter 2:13-21). "In the same way, you wives must accept the authority of your husbands. Then, even if some refuse to obey the Good News, your godly lives will speak to them without any words." (1 Peter 3:1).

The first response that God is looking for in all His children is to submit to those who are over us and to respect them. It does not say to just submit to and respect those who are kind and reasonable. No. It says to submit to ALL HUMAN AUTHORITY. It does not matter which party wins the election in November, the LORD is asking His children to submit to them and to respect them. It does not matter if your husband is good or bad, God is asking you to submit to him and to respect him. We will do this for the Lord's sake. This is how God wants all His holy children to respond.

HONOR ALL PEOPLE

I had to look up the definition of honor. The Oxford Dictionary says to honor is to show high respect and great esteem. I see no honor in our country. But God's kingdom is a kingdom of honor, so God's people must learn how to do this.

It starts at home with children honoring their parents. That means that all children must honor all parents. It does not matter if the parent is a good parent or not, the command is that every child will show his/her parents high respect and great esteem. This means to honor them with our thoughts, our words, and our actions.

Then wives and husbands must hold each other up with high respect and great esteem. "This is how the holy women of old made themselves beautiful. They put their trust in God and accepted the authority of their husbands. For instance, Sarah obeyed her husband, Abraham, and called him her master. You are her daughters when you do what is right without fear of what your husbands might do." (1 Peter 3:5-6). To obey our husbands shows them honor. To obey our parents shows them honor. To obey those in authority shows them honor. To obey God shows Him honor, too. Obedience is honor. Don't be afraid of what your husband will do. God knows. He is asking us to honor him.

"In the same way, you husbands must give honor to your wives. Treat your wife with understanding as you live together. She may be weaker than you are, but she is your equal partner in God's gift of new life. Treat her as you should so your prayers will not be hindered." (1 Peter 3:7). Husbands, even though you are the one in authority, try to understand your wife. Treat her the way you should. She is God's gift to you.

Honor those who are in authority. "Give to everyone what you owe them: Pay your taxes and government fees to those who collect them and give respect and honor to those who are in authority." (Romans 13:7). Do you know how hard it is to lead right now? God is asking every child of His to give honor (obedience) and respect to those who are in authority.

Finally, it says to honor all people. "Honor all people. Love the brotherhood. Fear God. Honor the king." (1 Peter 2:17 NKJV). God is asking His children to honor all people. This is the response He is looking for from us. We must begin to lift one another up in high respect and high esteem.

BE LOYAL and KIND

"My child, never forget the things I have taught you. Store My commandments in your heart. If you do this, you will live many years, and your life will be satisfying. Never let loyalty and kindness leave you! Tie them around your neck as a reminder. Write them deep within your heart. Then you will find favor with both God and people, and you will earn a good reputation." (Proverbs 3:1-4). If we want a satisfying life filled with favor from both God and people, and if we want to earn a good reputation, all we have to do is be kind to people -- all people – and be loyal.

I think we all know what being kind means, but what does it mean to be loyal? The Merriam-Webster Dictionary says that loyalty implies a faithfulness that is steadfast in the face of any temptation to renounce, desert, or betray. God is asking His people to be kind and loyal to all people. In the coming days we will have to be steadfast in the face of any temptation we will have to turn our back on people. God loves people. He wants to be kind to people, and He will use us to do it.

"Finally, all of you should be of one mind. Sympathize with each other. Love each other as brothers and sisters. Be tenderhearted and keep a humble attitude. Don't repay evil for evil. Don't retaliate with insults when people insult you. Instead, pay them back with a blessing. That is what God has called you to do, and He will grant you His blessing. For the Scriptures say,

> 'If you want to enjoy life
>   And see many happy days,
> Keep your tongue from speaking evil
>   And your lips from telling lies.
> Turn away from evil and do good.
>   Search for peace, and work to maintain it.
> The eyes of the LORD watch over those who do right,
>   And His ears are open to their prayers.
> But the LORD turns His face against those who do evil.'
> (1 Peter 3:8-12).

TAKE CARE OF THE POOR

God's eyes are always upon the poor and the needy and the orphans, widows and foreigners – especially in the household of faith. These are the people who are so easily oppressed. God wants to take care of them, and He is going to use us to do it. God wants there to be some equality, so He wants us to notice the real needs of others and to help meet those needs.

"Here is my advice: It would be good for you to finish what you started a year ago. Last year you were the first who wanted to give, and you were the first to begin doing it. Now you should finish what you started. Let the eagerness you showed in the beginning be matched now by your giving. Give in proportion to what you have. Whatever you give is acceptable if you give it eagerly. And give according to what you have, not what you don't have. I don't mean your giving should make life easy for others and hard for yourselves. I only mean that there should be some equality. Right now you have plenty and can help those who are in need. Later, they will have plenty and can share with you when you need it. In this way things will be equal. As the Scriptures say,

> 'Those who gathered a lot had nothing left over,
>   And those who gathered only a little had enough.'
> (2 Corinthians 8:10-15).

"Our people must learn to do good by meeting the urgent needs of others, then they will not be unproductive." (Titus 3:14).

Pay attention to the real needs of people. God wants His people to treat others the way that they would want others to treat them.

DO NOT COMPLAIN OR CRITICIZE

I don't think we understand what happens when we complain. "Don't grumble as some of them did, and then were destroyed by the angel of death. These things happened to them as examples for us. They were written down to warn us who live at the end of the age." (1 Corinthians 10:10-11). There is an angel of death that is loosed on us when we choose to complain. Let me give you some examples.

"Soon the people began to complain about their hardship, and the LORD heard everything they said. Then the LORD's anger blazed against them, and He sent a fire to rage among them, and He destroyed some of the people in the outskirts of the camp. Then the people screamed to Moses for help, and when he prayed to the LORD, the fire stopped." (Numbers 11:1-2). In the coming days, things are going to get hard. Don't let your heart focus on the hard things. Teach your mind to think on those things that are good and lovely and pure and holy. Let joy and thanksgiving enter your heart, even in the middle of hard times.

"Then the foreign rabble who were traveling with the Israelites began to crave the good things of Egypt. And the people of Israel also began to complain. 'Oh, for some meat?' they exclaimed. "We remember the fish we used to eat for free in Egypt. And we had all the cucumbers, melons, leeks, onions, and garlic we wanted. But now our appetites are gone. All we ever see is this manna.'" (Numbers 11:4-6). The complaining started with people who were not even God's people, but it wasn't long before they were all complaining about the food. "Moses heard all the families standing in the doorways of their tents whining, and the LORD became extremely angry." (Numbers 11:10).

"They kept on sinning against Him, rebelling against the Most High in the desert. They stubbornly tested God in their hearts, demanding the foods they craved. They even spoke against God Himself, saying, 'God can't give us food in the wilderness. Yes, He can strike a rock so water gushes out, but He can't give His people bread and meat.'"

"When the LORD heard them, He was furious. The fire of His wrath burned against Jacob. Yes, His anger rose against Israel, for THEY DID NOT BELIEVE GOD OR TRUST HIM TO CARE FOR THEM. But He commanded the skies to open; He opened the doors of heaven. He rained down manna for them to eat; He gave them bread from heaven. They ate the food of angels! God gave them all they could hold. He released the east wind in the heavens and guided the south wind by His mighty power. He rained down meat as thick as dust – birds as plentiful as the sand on the seashore! He caused the birds to fall within their camp and all around their tents. The people ate their fill. He gave them what they craved. But before they satisfied their craving, while the meat was yet in their mouths, the anger of God rose against them, and He killed their strongest men. He struck down the finest of Israel's young me." (Psalm 78:17-31).

You think this is just an Old Testament story – it doesn't apply to us, but it does. The same things that made God angry back then, make Him angry now. That is why 1 Corinthians 10:10-11 says, "These things happened to them as examples for us. They were written down to warn us who live at the end of the age." We, too, are going to want food that we use to have. We, too, are going to wonder if God will come through like He said He would. Take this story as a warning. No matter what happens, don't complain. Instead, in everything give thanks for this is the will of God for you in Christ Jesus. Trust God. He will take care of His people!

Then Miriam and Aaron complained against Moses. "While they were at Hazeroth, Miriam and Aaron criticized Moses because he had married a Cushite woman. They said, 'Has the LORD spoken only through Moses? Hasn't he spoken through us, too?' But the LORD heard them. (Now Moses was very humble – more humble than any other person on earth.) So Immediately the LORD called to Moses, Aaron, and Miriam and said, "Go out to the Tabernacle, all three of you!" So the three of them went to the Tabernacle. Then the LORD descended in the pillar of cloud and stood at the entrance of the Tabernacle. "Aaron and Miriam!" He called, and they stepped forward. And the LORD said to them, "Now listen to what I say:

> "If there were prophets among you, I, the LORD, would reveal Myself in visions. I would speak to them in dreams. But not with My servant Moses. Of all my house, he is the one I trust. I speak to him face to face, clearly, and not in riddles! He sees the LORD as He is. So why were you not afraid to criticize My servant Moses?"

The LORD was very angry with them, and He departed. As the cloud moved from above the Tabernacle, there stood Miriam, her skin as white as snow from leprosy. When Aaron saw what had happened to her, he cried out to Moses, "Oh, my master! Please don't punish us for this sin we have so foolishly committed. Don't let her be like a stillborn baby, already decayed at birth."

So Moses cried out to the LORD, "Oh God, I beg You, please heal her!" But the LORD said to Moses, "If her father had done nothing more than spit in her face, wouldn't she be defiled for seven days? So keep her outside of the camp for seven days, and after that she may be accepted back." (Numbers 12:1-14).

We cannot criticize people, especially the people God has chosen to lead us. After Moses sent the twelve spies into the promised land to scope it out and they came back with a bad report, and the people began weeping. "Then the whole community began weeping aloud, and they cried all night. Their voices rose in a great chorus of protest against Moses and Aaron. 'If only we had died in Egypt, or even here in the wilderness!' they complained." "Why is the LORD taking us to this country only to have us die in battle? Wouldn't it be better for us to return to Egypt?" Then they plotted among themselves, "Let's choose a new leader and go back to Egypt." (Numbers 14:1-4).

"The whole community began to talk about stoning Joshua and Caleb. Then the glorious presence of the LORD appeared to all the Israelites at the Tabernacle. And the LORD said to Moses, "How long will these people treat Me with contempt? WILL THEY NEVER BELIEVE ME, even after all the miraculous signs I have done among them? I will disown them and destroy them with a plague. Then I will make you into a nation greater and mightier than they are!" (Numbers 14:10-12).

When the people rebelled against Moses and Aaron and Joshua and Caleb, they were really rebelling against God. God wanted to destroy the whole nation, but Moses talked Him out of it saying, "In keeping with Your magnificent, unfailing love, please pardon the sins of this people, just as you have forgiven them ever since they left Egypt." (Numbers 14:19). Moses appealed to God's merciful nature, and God heard him, but God then said, "Because your men explored the land for forty days, you must wander in the wilderness for forty years – a year for each day, suffering the consequences of your sins. THEN YOU WILL DISCOVER WHAT IT IS LIKE TO HAVE ME FOR AN ENEMY. I, the LORD have spoken! I will certainly do these things to every member of the community who has conspired against Me. They will be destroyed here in this wilderness, and here they will die!" Then "the ten men Moses had sent to explore the land – the ones who incited rebellion against the LORD with their bad report – were struck dead with a plague before the LORD. Of the twelve who had explored the land, only Joshua and Caleb remained alive." (Numbers 14:34-38).

We must stay unified, and we cannot do that if we complain and criticize each other. "Dear friends, you always followed my instructions when I was with you. And now that I am away, it is even more important. Work hard to show the results of your salvation, obeying God with deep reverence and fear. For God is working in you, giving you the desire and the power to do what pleases Him. Do everything without complaining and arguing, so that no one can criticize you. Live clean, innocent lives as children of God, shining like bright lights in a world full of crooked and perverse people." (Philippians 2:12-15). God is giving us the desire and the power to do everything without complaining and arguing. In the coming days, God's holy people will shine like the stars in the heavens as we show forth the Word of Life.

REJOICE and GIVE THANKS

It doesn't even make sense to the natural mind to give thanks in all circumstances, but that is the response God is looking for – ALWAYS. "Always be joyful. Never stop praying. Be thankful in all circumstances, for this is God's will for you who belong to Christ." (1 Thessalonians 5:16-18).

To be thankful in all circumstances. Think about what you are going through right now. Is your heart rejoicing? Is it giving thanks? If it is not, run to God. Be real. Open your heart wide. Let Him hold you. Then thank Him. Declare all the great things He has done for you. Let a spirit of thanksgiving and praise enter your heart. Rejoice!

"Always be full of joy in the Lord. I say it again – rejoice! Let everyone see that you are considerate in all you do. Remember, the Lord is coming soon. Don't worry about anything; instead, pray about everything. Tell God what you need and thank Him for what He has done. Then you will experience God's peace, which exceeds anything we can understand. His peace will guard your hearts and minds as you live in Christ Jesus." PEACE! That is our inheritance. It will guard our hearts and minds as we live in Christ Jesus.

"And now, dear brothers and sisters, one final thing. Fix your thoughts on what is true, and honorable, and right, and pure, and lovely, and admirable. THINK ABOUT THINGS that are excellent and worthy of praise. Keep putting into practice all you learned and received from me – everything you heard from me and saw me doing. Then the God of peace will be with you." (Philippians 4:4-9). "For I HAVE LEARNED HOW TO BE CONTENT with whatever I have. I know how to live on almost nothing or with everything. I have learned the secret of living in every situation, whether it is with a full stomach or empty, with plenty or little. For I can do everything through Christ, who gives me strength." (Philippians 4:11-13).

To be able to rejoice and give thanks, we must guard our thoughts and learn to be content in all circumstances. To do that, we must keep running to God to find refuge in Him. We must keep holding onto the hope that is set before us. We can trust God. He is trustworthy. When we choose to thank Him in all circumstances, we are saying, "God, we trust you. Now, You are going to have to take care of us."

God is in complete control. Trust it. "And we know that God causes everything to work together for the good of those who love God and are called according to His purpose for them. For God knew His people in advance, and He chose them to become like His Son, so that His Son would be the firstborn among many brothers and sisters." (Romans 8:28-29). Everything that is happening to us is because it is going to train us to be like Jesus. "The LORD directs the steps of the godly. He delights in every detail of their live. Though they stumble, they will never fall, for the LORD holds them by the hand." (Psalm 37:23-24). EVERY DETAIL! Trust it.

Then we will get to a point when we can say, along with James, "Dear brothers and sisters, when troubles of any kind come your way, consider it an opportunity for great joy. For you know that when your faith is tested, your endurance has a chance to grow. So let it grow, for when your endurance is fully developed, you will be perfect and complete, needing nothing." (James 1:2-4).

BE HUMBLE and GENTLE and PATIENT

"Therefore, I, a prisoner for serving the Lord, beg you to lead a life worthy of your calling, for you have been called by God. Always be humble and gentle. Be patient with each other, making allowance for each other's faults because of your love. Make every effort to keep yourselves united in the Spirit, binding yourselves together with peace. For there is one body and one Spirit, just as you have been called to one glorious hope for the future." (Ephesians 4:1-4).

Jesus is humble and gentle and patient and kind, and He is calling us to be the same. He wants unity. He wants peace. When we humble ourselves, we can be gentle and patient and kind. We can make allowances for each other's faults. We can make peace with others because it doesn't have to be my way.

This is so foreign to the way we have done things in the past. We want things to be done right, and we think we know what that right way is, but God wants peace and unity. He wants kindness. The only way we can do this is if we make ourselves lower than other people. We are called to think of others as more important than ourselves. We are called to yield and to submit. This brings peace and it brings unity. So, we must: "Get rid of all bitterness, rage, anger, harsh words, and slander, as well as all types of evil behavior. Instead, be kind to each other, tenderhearted, forgiving one another, just as God through Christ has forgiven you." (Ephesians 4:31-32).

Then Jesus said to them, "Come to Me, all of you who are weary and carry heavy burdens, and I will give you rest. Take My yoke upon you. Let Me teach you, because I am humble and gentle at heart, and you will find rest for your souls. For My yoke is easy to bear, and the burden I give you is light." (Matthew 11:28-30). Wow! When we come to Jesus and let Him teach us how to be humble and gentle at heart, we will find rest for our souls. All our heavy burdens will be gone. This yoke of humility is easy to bear, and its burden is light. Humble. Gentle. Rest. God is good!

SPEAK THE TRUTH and LOVE PEOPLE

With all this yielding and submitting and being humble and gentle and kind, we would think that we would not make a difference, things would not change, but it will. The one thing God is asking His people to do is speak the truth in love.

"Now these are the gifts Christ gave to the church: the apostles, the prophets, the evangelists, and the pastors and teachers. Their responsibility is to equip God's people to do His work and build up the church, the body of Christ. This will continue until we all come to such unity in our faith and knowledge of God's Son that we will be mature in the Lord, measuring up to the full and complete standard of Christ."

"Then we will no longer be immature like children. We won't be tossed and blown about by every wind of new teaching. We will not be influenced when people try to trick us with lies so clever they sound like the truth. Instead, we will SPEAK THE TRUTH IN LOVE, growing in every way more and more like Christ, who is the head of His body, the church. He makes the whole body fit together perfectly. As each part does its own special work, it helps the other parts grow, so that the whole body is healthy and growing and full of love." (Ephesians 4:11-16).

When we choose to be humble and gentle and patient and kind, thinking of others as more important than ourselves, and yet, we still speak the truth in love, something magical happens. We become joined together as one. Each part of God's body is important, and we all come together to make a holy dwelling place for God's Spirit. We will continue in this way until we all come to such a unity in our faith and knowledge of God's Son that we will be mature in the Lord, measuring up to the full and complete standard of Christ. Wow!

But it is only the truth that will set us free, so we must not withhold the truth from anyone. God's Word is Truth. "The Spirit alone gives eternal life. Human effort accomplishes nothing. And the very Words I have spoken to you are Spirit and life." (John 6:63). The Word of God will bring life. It will be seed planted in fertile soil that will bring forth an abundant harvest of righteousness. We must sew seed and love people. It is up to God to do the rest. At just the right time God will make things happen.

"For your land will be overgrown with thorns and briers. Your joyful homes and happy towns will be gone. The palace and the city will be deserted, and busy towns will be empty. Wild donkeys will frolic, and flocks will graze in the empty forts and watchtowers UNTIL AT LAST the Spirit is poured out on us from heaven. Then the wilderness will become a fertile field, and the fertile field will yield bountiful crops."

"Justice will rule in the wilderness and righteousness in the fertile field. And this righteousness will bring peace. Yes, it will bring quietness and confidence forever. My people will live in safety, quietly at home. They will be at rest. Even if the forest should be destroyed and the city torn down, the LORD will greatly bless His people. WHEREVER THEY PLANT SEED, bountiful crops will spring up. Their cattle and donkeys will graze freely." (Isaiah 32:13-20).

There will come a time that wherever we plant seed (the Word of God), bountiful crops will spring up. We cannot withhold the truth. God is asking us to speak the truth and to love people – no matter the response.

So, these are the responses God is looking for in His people. We will be kind and loyal. We will honor and respect all people. We will submit to all authority for the Lord's sake. We will be humble and gentle and patient and kind. We will give thanks in every circumstance. We will rejoice always. And we will speak the truth and love people – all people. We will come to a place where we will be one. Unified. "One body and one Spirit, just as we have been called to one glorious hope for the future. There is one Lord, one faith, one baptism, one God and Father of all, who is over all, in all, and living through all." (Ephesians 4:4-6). God Himself will make this happen.

"He is so rich in kindness and grace that He purchased our freedom with the blood of His Son and forgave our sins. He has showered His kindness on us, along with all wisdom and understanding. God has NOW revealed to us His mysterious will regarding Christ – which is to fulfill His own good plan. And this is the plan: AT THE RIGHT TIME He will bring everything together under the authority of Christ – everything in heaven and on earth. Furthermore, because we are united with Christ, we have received an inheritance from God, for He chose us in advance, and He makes everything work out according to His plan." (Ephesians 1:7-11). Trust it!

12. OPEN YOUR MOUTH WIDE AND I WILL FILL IT WITH GOOD THINGS.

We have no idea what happens in the spirit realm when we speak. Life. Death. Blessings. Curses. God sends things our way when we open our mouth. We speak things into existence. "Death and life are in the power of the tongue. And those who love it will eat its fruit." (Proverbs 18:21). We will all eat the fruit of what we say.

"If you claim to be religious but don't control your tongue, you are fooling yourself, and your religion is worthless." (James 1:26). Our religion is worthless if our tongue is not tamed. "A tiny spark can set a great forest on fire. And among all the parts of the body, the tongue is a flame of fire. It is a whole world of wickedness, corrupting your entire body. It can set your whole life on fire, for it is set on fire by hell itself." (James 3:5-6). We can all tell if we belong to God or not just by listening to what we say. Are we grumbling and complaining or are we praising God? Do we dishonor, disrespect, slander and mock, or do we honor and respect people? Do we encourage or discourage? The words we speak give us away.

"Indeed, we all make mistakes. For if we could control our tongues, we would be perfect and could also control ourselves in every other way." (James 3:2). If we could control the tongue, we could control our whole body, but we can't. "People can tame all kinds of animals, birds, reptiles, and fish, but no one can tame the tongue. It is restless and evil, full of deadly poison. Sometimes it praises our Lord and Father, and sometimes it curses those who have been made in the image of God. And so blessing and cursing come pouring out of the same mouth. Surely, my brothers and sisters, this is not right! Does a spring of water bubble out with both fresh water and bitter water? Does a fig tree produce olives, or a grapevine produce figs? No, and you can't draw fresh water from a salty spring." (James 3:7-12). We have all been there, fresh water and bitter water coming out of the same spring. It is not right.

"A tree is identified by its fruit. If a tree is good, its fruit will be good. If a tree is bad, its fruit will be bad. You brood of snakes! How could evil men like you speak what is good and right? For WHATEVER IS IN YOUR HEART DETERMINES WHAT YOU SAY. A good person produces good things from the treasury of a good heart, and an evil person produces evil things from the treasury of an evil heart. And I tell you this, you must give an account on judgment day for every idle word you speak. The words you say will either acquit you or condemn you." (Matthew 12:33-37).

We will be judged by every idle word we have ever spoken on judgment day. Our words will either acquit us or condemn us. But it is actually our HEART that is speaking. "The human heart is the most deceitful of all things, and desperately wicked. Who really knows how bad it is? But I, the LORD, search all hearts and examine secret motives. I give all people their due rewards, according to what their actions deserve." (Jeremiah 17:9-10). It is out of this desperately wicked, deceitful heart that we speak words. No wonder our tongue is a flame of fire, a whole world of wickedness that corrupts our entire body. So, what do we do?

We turn to God. We ask Him to do for us what we cannot do for ourselves. "Create in me a clean heart, O God. Renew a loyal spirit within me." (Psalm 51:10). Only God can change a heart, so we turn to Him to do what He wants to do already. Then we listen to what He is asking us to do, and we obey. Psalm 81 gives us insight into how to tame this restless tongue that is so full of evil and deadly poison.

Sing praises to God, our strength.
   Sing to the God of Jacob.
Sing! Beat the tambourine.
   Play the sweet lyre and the harp.
Blow the ram's horn at new moon,
   and again at full moon to call a festival!
For this is required by the decrees of Israel;
   It is a regulation of the God of Jacob.
He made it a law for Israel
   When He attacked Egypt to set us free. (Psalm 81:1-5).

There is a law written in the heavenly realms that we will praise God. Praise is required. It is a regulation. If we want God to come and set us free, we will praise Him.

I heard an unknown voice say,

> "Now I will take the load from your shoulders;
> I will free your hands from their heavy tasks.
> You cried to Me in trouble, and I saved you;
> I answered out of the thundercloud
> and TESTED YOUR FAITH when there was no water at Meribah."
> (Psalm 81:5-7).

When we choose to praise God in the middle of hard circumstances, God takes the load from our shoulders and frees our hands from heavy tasks. Try it! In the middle of whatever hard thing that is happening, stop what you are doing, turn to God, and begin worshiping Him. Praise Him. Tell of the awesome things He has done. See what happens in your heart. It is spectacular! But don't think we won't be tested in this. God said, "And I tested your faith when there was no water at Meribah." (Psalm 81:7). Are we still going to praise God when there is no water – or whatever else He decides to take from us???

PRAISE GOD NO MATTER WHAT HAPPENS. What does that have to do with the words that we speak? Listen to what Psalm 81 says next.

"Listen to Me, O My people, while I give you stern warnings. O Israel, if you would only listen to Me! (Praise Me!) You must never have a foreign god; you must not bow down before a false god. For it was I, the LORD your God, who rescued you from the land of Egypt. Open your mouth wide, and I will fill it with good things." (Psalm 81:8-10). Oh, my goodness! If we will do this little thing – praise God, God will fill our mouth with good things. Every other word that we speak will be life and health and hope because God will put those words there. When we choose to praise God even in the hardest circumstance – like having no water, He makes something happen in our heart that causes it to line up with His heart. Then we can speak good things. We will be a good tree that bears good fruit. Wow! This is so simple. "Sing praises to God, our strength!" He does the rest.

"But no, My people wouldn't listen. Israel did not want Me around. So I let them follow their own stubborn desires, living according to their own ideas." (Psalm 81:11-12). What? We won't do this? It is so simple. Praise God! But no. I think we are going to do whatever we want to do - follow whatever god we want to follow, say whatever words we want to say.

"Oh, that My people would listen to Me! Oh, that Israel would follow Me, walking in My paths! How quickly I would then subdue their enemies! How soon My hands would be upon their foes! Those who hate the LORD would cringe before Him; they would be doomed forever. But I would feed you with the finest wheat. I would satisfy you with wild honey from the rock." (Psalm 81:13-16).

If only we would listen. If only we would obey. If only we would follow God, walking in His paths. God would do the rest. He would destroy our enemies, and He would feed us with the finest wheat and honey. The words that we speak would be sweet and nourishing. If only...

God's people will be a people of praise and thanksgiving. The rest of the world will not.

13. BE READY TO SUFFER

No one wants to talk about suffering. Everyone wants the rapture to happen before everything gets bad, but that is not what I am seeing.

"Look, I am sending you out as sheep among wolves. So be as shrewd as snakes and harmless as doves. But beware! For you will be handed over to the courts and will be flogged with whips in the synagogues. You will stand trial before governors and kings because you are My followers. But this will be your opportunity to tell the rulers and other unbelievers about Me. When you are arrested, don't worry about how to respond or what to say. God will give you the right words at the right time. For it is not you who will be speaking – it will be the Spirit of your Father speaking through you."

"A brother will betray his brother to death, a father will betray his own child, and children will rebel against their parents and cause them to be killed. And ALL NATIONS WILL HATE YOU because you are my followers. But everyone who endures to the end will be saved. When you are persecuted in one town, flee to the next. I tell you the truth, the Son of Man will return before you have reached all the towns of Israel."

"Students are not greater than their teacher, and slaves are not greater than their master. Students are to be like their teacher, and slaves are to be like their master. And since I, the master of the household, have been called the prince of demons, the members of My household will be called by even worse names!"

"But don't be afraid of those who threaten you. For the time is coming when everything that is covered will be revealed, and all that is secret will be made known to all. What I tell you now in the darkness, shout abroad when daybreak comes. What I whisper in your ear, shout from the house tops for all to hear!"

"Don't be afraid of those who want to kill your body; they cannot touch your soul. Fear only God, who can destroy both soul and body in hell. What is the price of two sparrows – one copper coin? But not a single sparrow can fall to the ground without your Father knowing it. And the very hairs on your head are all numbered. So don't be afraid; you are more valuable to God than a whole flock of sparrows."

"Everyone who acknowledges Me publicly here on earth, I will also acknowledge before My Father in heaven. But everyone who denies Me here on earth, I will also deny before My Father in heaven."

"Don't imagine that I came to bring peace to the earth! I came not to bring peace, but a sword.

> 'I have come to set a man against his father,
>   a daughter against her mother,
> and a daughter-in-law against her mother-in-law.
>   Your enemies will be right in your own household!'

"If you love your father or mother more than you love Me, you are not worthy of being mine; or if you love your son or daughter more than Me, you are not worthy of being mine. If you refuse to take up your cross and follow Me, you are not worthy of being mine. If you cling to your life, you will lose it; but if you give up your life for Me, you will find it."

"Anyone who receives you receives Me, and anyone who receives Me receives the Father who sent Me. If you receive a prophet as one who speaks for God, you will be given the same reward as a prophet. And if you receive righteous people because of their righteousness, you will be given a reward like theirs. And if you give even a cup of cold water to one of the least of My followers, you will surely be rewarded." (Matthew 10:16-42).

According to this passage, all of God's people will be hated. People will betray us, threaten us, call us names, persecute us, throw us into prison, and kill us. This is all part of God's plan. He tells us what is going to happen in advance so that we will not get discouraged and fall away when it does happen.

What God wants us to do when all these things happen is to not be afraid. We are so important to God! He is going to take care of us. What He tells us in the darkness, He wants us to shout in the daylight. He wants us to acknowledge Him publicly. We can't hide. We can't pretend we don't know Him because we do know Him. He wants us to love Him more than we love any other person. He wants us to not be ashamed of Him. He wants us to take up our cross (whatever cross that may be) and follow Him. When Jesus took up His cross, it led Him into a mob who shouted, "Crucify Him!" This world is not our home. We are only passing through.

"Now we live with great expectation, and we have a priceless inheritance – an inheritance that is kept in heaven for you, pure and undefiled, beyond the reach of change and decay. And through your faith, GOD IS PROTECTING YOU BY HIS POWER until you receive this salvation, which is ready to be revealed on the last day for all to see." (1 Peter 1:3-5). Through all that we go through, God will protect us by His mighty power until we receive our salvation in its fullness.

"So be truly glad. There is wonderful joy ahead, even though you must endure many trials for a little while. These trials will show that your faith is genuine. It is being tested as fire tests and purifies gold – though your faith is far more precious than mere gold. So when your faith remains strong through many trials, it will bring you much praise and glory and honor on the day when Jesus Christ is revealed to the whole world."

"You love Him even though you have never seen Him. Though you do not see Him now, you trust Him; and you rejoice with a glorious, inexpressible joy. The reward for trusting Him will be the salvation of your souls." (1 Peter 1:6-9).

We will all be tested in the coming days. These trials will purify us and refine us. We will trust God, and in the middle of all these unimaginable trials, God will shower us with inexpressible joy. That doesn't even make sense, but that is what is going to happen.

"So prepare your MINDS for action and exercise self-control. Put all your hope in the gracious salvation that will come to you when Jesus Christ is revealed to the world. So you must live as God's obedient children. Don't slip back into your old ways of living to satisfy your own desires. You didn't know any better then. But now you must be holy in everything you do, just as God who chose you is holy. For the scriptures say, "You must be holy because I am holy."

"And remember that the heavenly Father to whom you pray has no favorites. He will judge or reward you according to what you do. So you must live in reverent fear of Him during your time here as "temporary residents." (1 Peter 1:13).

We must start by preparing our MINDS. God told us what would happen so that we would be prepared. Then we must live as OBEDIENT CHILDREN. We didn't know what we were doing before, but now we do. God is calling His children to be HOLY just as He is holy, and He will reward us for it, but it will not be easy.

"So then, since Christ suffered physical pain, you must arm yourselves with the same attitude He had, and be ready to suffer, too." (1 Peter 4:1). Physical pain? I don't know about you, but this does not sound fun. It doesn't even feel like something I can do, but God is asking us right now to ARM OURSELVES WITH THE SAME ATTITUDE Christ had. He was ready to suffer for us. Are we ready to suffer for Him?

I don't know if I am ready to suffer for Jesus, but I can tell you this – my eyes are on Him. I am listening to what He is saying. And I am trying to obey Him in every area of my life. I am trying to arm myself with the same attitude He had. He was willing. I am willing, too.

"For if you have suffered physically for Christ, you have finished with sin. You won't spend the rest of your lives chasing your own desires, but you will be anxious to do the will of God." (1 Peter 4:1-2). If we suffer physically for Jesus, we will be done with sin. Is this what it takes to be done with sin? I don't know, but I am listening to what He is saying.

In Philippians Paul says, "I want to know Christ and experience the mighty power that raised Him from the dead. I want to suffer with Him, sharing in His death, so that one way or another I will experience the resurrection from the dead!" (Philippians 3:10-11). I want to know Christ, too. I think suffering is a part of knowing Christ. I just don't know if I am prepared for what that might mean. "So prepare your minds for action and exercise self-control. Put all your hope in the gracious salvation that will come to you when Jesus Christ is revealed to the world." (1 Peter 1:13).

I am preparing my mind for action and setting my hope in the gracious salvation that comes from Jesus. God is going to have to do the rest. I trust that He will when the time comes. He will supply all that I need to do whatever He is asking me to do. For now, I am listening to what He is saying and setting my hope in Him. I am preparing my mind to suffer. When the time comes, I will run to God for refuge and lay hold of the HOPE that is set before me. That hope is a strong and trustworthy anchor for my soul. It leads us through the curtain into God's inner sanctuary. Jesus has already gone in there for us. He will make sure we make it safely.

14. GOD WILL MAKE US AN IMMOVABLE ROCK.

When I look at the big, good plan of God, I cannot see any way that we will be able to make it in the natural. It will be too big and too hard, but when I listen to what He is going to do for us in the spiritual, I realize that our heart will not falter. God is going to fight for us. He will defeat every enemy. We will be victorious.

"This message concerning the fate of Israel came from the LORD: 'This message is from the LORD, who stretched out the heavens, laid the foundations of the earth, and formed the human spirit. I will make Jerusalem like an intoxicating drink that makes the nearby nations stagger when they send their armies to besiege Jerusalem and Judah. On that day I will make Jerusalem an immovable rock. All the nations will gather against it to try to move it, but they will only hurt themselves.'"

"On that day," says the LORD, "I will cause every horse to panic and every rider to lose his nerve. I will watch over the people of Judah, but I will blind all the horses of their enemies. And the clans of Judah will say to themselves, 'The people of Jerusalem have found strength in the LORD of Heaven's Armies, their God.'"

"On that day I will make the clans of Judah like a flame that sets a woodpile ablaze or like a burning torch among sheaves of grain. They will burn up all the neighboring nations right and left, while the people of Jerusalem remain secure."

"The LORD will give victory to the rest of Judah first, before Jerusalem, so that the people of Jerusalem and the royal line of David will not have greater honor than the rest of Judah. On that day the LORD will defend the people of Jerusalem: the weakest among them will be as mighty as

King David! And the royal descendants will be like God, like the angel of the LORD who goes before them! For on that day, I will begin to destroy all the nations that come against Jerusalem." (Zechariah 12:1-9).

We will remain secure while all the rest of the world is burned up. We will find strength in our God. We will be immoveable. The weakest among us will be as mighty as King David. And the royal descendants will be like God – like the angel of the LORD who goes before us. Wow! Do we even know what that means?!

> "Is anyone thirsty?
> Come and drink –
> Even if you have no money!
> Come, take your choice of wine or milk –
> It's all free!
> Why spend your money on food that does not give you strength?
> Why pay for food that does you no good?
> Listen to Me, and you will eat what is good.
> You will enjoy the finest food."

"Come to Me with your ears wide open. Listen, and you will find life. I will make an everlasting covenant with you. I will give you all the unfailing love I promised to David. See how I used Him to display My power among the peoples. I made him a leader among the nations. You also will command nations you do not know, and peoples unknown to you will come running to obey, because I, the LORD your God, the Holy One of Israel, have made you glorious." (Isaiah 55:1-5).

God is offering this free gift to all people! Is anyone thirsty, come and drink – even if you have no money. This promise is for all. All we must do is come. Listen to what the LORD is saying and you, too, will eat what is good. Come with your ears wide open, and you will find life. Then God will make an everlasting covenant with you. He will give you all the unfailing love that He promised to David. He will then use you to display His power among the peoples. You, too, will command nations you do not know, and peoples unknown to you will come running to obey, because God will make you glorious!

We are all standing in the valley of decision and God is calling our name.

Will we listen?

"Seek the LORD while you can find Him. Call on Him now while He is near. Let the wicked change their ways and banish the very thought of doing wrong. Let them turn to the LORD that He may have mercy on them. Yes, turn to our God, for He will forgive generously."

"My thoughts are nothing like your thoughts," says the LORD. "And My ways are far beyond anything you could imagine. For just as the heavens are higher than the earth, so My ways are higher than your ways and My thoughts higher than your thoughts."

"The rain and snow come down from the heavens and stay on the ground to water the earth. They cause the grain to grow, producing seed for the farmer and bread for the hungry. It is the same with My Word. I send it out, and it always produces fruit. It will accomplish all I want it to, and it will prosper everywhere I send it. You will live in joy and peace. The mountains and hills will burst into song, and the trees of the field will clap their hands! Where once there were thorns, cypress trees will grow. Where nettles grew, myrtles will sprout up. These events will bring great honor to the LORD's name: they will be an everlasting sign of His power and love." (Isaiah 55:6-13).

Right now, we must seek God while we can find Him and call on Him while He is near. Let us turn to God and banish every thought of doing wrong. He WILL forgive generously. The mountains and hills will burst into song! The trees of the field will clap their hands! Thorns and nettles will disappear, and cypress trees and myrtles will grow. God will cause all these things to happen.

"I have created the blacksmith who fans the coals beneath the forge and makes the weapons of destruction. And I have created the armies that destroy. But in that coming day no weapon turned against you will succeed. You will silence every voice raised up to accuse you. These benefits are enjoyed by the servants of the LORD; their vindication will come from Me. I, the LORD, have spoken!" (Isaiah 54:16-17).

"Sing, O childless woman, you who have never given birth! Break into loud and joyful song, O Jerusalem, you who have never been in labor. For the desolate woman now has more children than the woman who lives with her husband," says the LORD.

"Enlarge your house; build an addition. Spread out your home and spare no expense. For you will soon be bursting at the seams. Your descendants will occupy other nations and resettle the ruined cities."

"Fear not; you will no longer live in shame. Don't be afraid; there is no more disgrace for you. You will no longer remember the shame of your youth and the sorrows of widowhood. For your Creator will be your husband, the LORD of Heaven's Armies is His name! He is your Redeemer, the Holy One of Israel, the God of all the earth."

"For the LORD has called you back from your grief – as though you were a young wife abandoned by her husband," says your God. "For a brief moment I abandoned you, but with great compassion I will take you back. In a burst of anger, I turned My face away for a little while. But with everlasting love I will have compassion on you," says the LORD, your Redeemer.

"Just as I swore in the time of Noah that I would never again let a flood cover the earth, now I swear that I will never again be angry and punish you. For the mountains may move and the hills disappear, but even then My faithful love for you will remain. My covenant of blessing will never be broken," says the LORD, who has mercy on you.

"O storm-battered city, troubled and desolate! I will rebuild you with precious jewels and make your foundations from lapis lazuli. I will make your towers of sparkling rubies, your gates of shining gems, and your walls of precious stones. I will teach all your children, and they will enjoy great peace. You will be secure under a government that is just and fair. Your enemies will stay far away. You will live in peace, and terror will not come near. If any nation comes to fight you, it is not because I sent them. Whoever attacks you will go down in defeat." (Isaiah 54:1-15).

We do not have to worry about what is going to happen. God Himself is coming to fight for us. He is making a covenant with us that can never be broken. He will bless His people. No weapon that is formed against us will ever prosper, and we will silence every voice that rises up to accuse us. God will rebuild our storm-battered city with precious jewels, and we will live securely under a government (in our own heart) that is just and fair. Our enemies will stay far away, and we will live in peace – terror will not come near.

God will make us immoveable, even in the face of suffering and persecution. We will have joy and peace. The mountains and the hills will burst into song. The trees of the fields will clap their hands. These events will bring great honor to the LORD's name; they will be an everlasting sign of His power and love.

15. GOD WILL POUR OUT A SPIRIT OF GRACE AND PRAYER.

In December 2023, God gave me a Word. He said, "The end of the world is coming soon. Therefore, be earnest and disciplined in your prayers." (1 Peter 4:7). Prayer! We will partner with God in what is about to happen. This concerned me because just like everything else, I wondered, "Will we get it right?" Then I saw this...

"On that day the LORD will defend the people of Jerusalem; the weakest among them will be as mighty as King David! And the royal descendants will be like God, like the angel of the LORD who goes before them! For on that day, I will begin to destroy all the nations that come against Jerusalem. Then I will POUR OUT A SPIRIT OF GRACE AND PRAYER on the family of David and on the people of Jerusalem." (Zechariah 12:8-10).

It is God's Spirit that will orchestrate our prayer life. We must trust it. I want you to hear what our Father says about prayer. May we all have eyes to see, ears to hear, and a heart to understand what He is saying.

"At times I might shut up the heavens so that no rain falls, or command grasshoppers to devour your crops, or send plagues among you. Then if My people who are called by My name will humble themselves and pray and seek My face and turn from their wicked ways, I will hear from heaven and will forgive their sins and restore their land. My eyes will be open and My ears attentive to every prayer made in this place. For I have chosen this Temple and set it apart to be holy – a place where My name will be honored forever. I will always watch over it, for it is dear to My heart." (2 Chronicles 7:13-16).

God sometimes shuts up the heavens so that no rain falls or sends grasshoppers or plagues for this reason...

> "Then if My people who are called by My name will HUMBLE THEMSELVES and PRAY and SEEK MY FACE and TURN FROM THEIR WICKED WAYS, then I will hear from heaven and will forgive their sins and restore their land." (2 Chronicles 7:14).

God sends things our way so that we will be humbled. Then we will pray and seek His face and turn from our wicked ways. That is what God is after. He wants repentance. It will not happen unless things get hard. So let us let every hard circumstance humble us so that we have to pray and seek God's face. Let every hard circumstance cause us to examine our hearts to see if there is any wicked way in us so that we can turn from it. If we do these things, God will forgive our sins and restore our land.

THEN God's eyes will be open and His ears attentive to every prayer we make. Did you hear that? We will be a chosen vessel – a Temple – that God has set apart as holy – a place where His name will be honored forever. We will be dear to His heart, and He will always watch over us. Can you see that? If we will HUMBLE ourselves and PRAY and SEEK HIS FACE and TURN FROM OUR WICKED WAYS, we will be holy. Our prayers will then be holy because our sins will be forgiven. There will no longer be anything that gets in the way of us reaching the heart of our Father. We will be in a position to pray, and God will be in a position to listen. We will then ask God to do for His people what He wants to do anyway. Wow!

So, what does the Father want to do for all His children? He wants us to turn to Him. He wants us to know Him. He wants us to trust Him. He wants us to believe what He says and to obey. He wants us to lay our burdens down. He wants us to love one another. He wants us to care for the poor and needy. He wants us to be thankful and grateful. He wants us to be holy – completely set apart unto Him. When we look around, we don't see many people who are there yet, so we pray.

GOD WILL GIVE US WHAT WE ASK FOR. TRUST IT!

"What is causing the quarrels and fights among you? Don't they come from the evil desires at war within you? You want what you don't have, so you scheme and kill to get it. You are jealous of what others have, but you can't get it, so you fight and wage war to take it away from them. Yet you don't have what you want because you don't ask God for it. And even when you ask, you don't get it because your motive are all wrong – you want only what will bring you pleasure." (James 4:1-3).

From this passage we can see that we will not get what we ask for if we are asking only for things that will bring us pleasure. When we are proud or greedy or covetous or jealous, we will not get anything from God. But, if we get rid of these spirits that move us toward evil desires, we will be in a position to pray prayers that God WILL ANSWER.

"If you remain in Me and My words remain in you, you may ask for anything you want, and it will be granted! When you produce much fruit you are My TRUE DISCIPLES. This brings great glory to My Father." (John 15:7-8).

When we are in Jesus and His words are in us, we will ask things that bring Him glory. Of course He is going to grant it! We will partner with Jesus! "You didn't choose Me. I chose you. I appointed you to go and produce lasting fruit, so that the Father will give you whatever you ask for, using My name. This is My command: Love each other." (John 15:16-17). FRUIT! LASTING FRUIT! When we live in Jesus and Jesus lives in us, we will be full of love, joy, peace, patience, kindness, goodness, faithfulness, gentleness, and self-control. Love will move us, and it will move us in our prayers.

God wants us to have this kind of lasting fruit in our lives SO THAT God will give us whatever we ask for. Oh, my goodness! God will answer all the prayers of His holy people – His true disciples. We have the honor and the privilege of standing in the gap for people. He will hear and answer! Look around! It is time to pray!

PRAY FOR YOUR ALL PEOPLE

God wants us to pray for all people. We cannot think in our hearts that there are some people worthy of our prayers and others who are not.

"I urge you, first of all, to pray for all people. Ask God to help them; intercede on their behalf and give thanks for them. Pray this way for kings and all who are in authority so that we can live peaceful and quiet lives marked by godliness and dignity. This is good and pleases God our Savior, who wants everyone to be saved and to understand the truth. For,

> There is one God and one Mediator who can reconcile God and humanity – the man Christ Jesus. He gave His life to purchase freedom for everyone.

This is the message God gave to the world at JUST THE RIGHT TIME." (1 Timothy 2:1-6).

Jesus gave His life to purchase freedom for everyone. That is why we cannot pick and choose who we pray for. God wants everyone to be saved and to understand the truth. It pleases Him when we pray for people – even those who oppose us.

"You have heard the law that says, 'Love your neighbor and hate your enemy. But I say, love your enemies! Pray for those who persecute you! In that way, you will be acting as true children of your Father in heaven. For He gives His sunlight to both the evil and the good, and He sends rain on the just and the unjust alike. If you love only those who love you, what reward is there for that? Even corrupt tax collectors do that much. If you are kind only to your friends, how are you different from anyone else? Even pagans do that. But you are to be perfect, even as your Father in heaven is perfect." (Matthew 5:43-48).

When we choose to thank God for our enemies and to ask Him to help them before we start to pray, it puts us on the same side. We are for them, not against them. That makes all the difference in the world. Then we can ask God what we need to pray so that they can come to know Him, too.

When we choose to thank God for kings and all who are in authority and to ask God to help them before we begin to intercede on their behalf, it puts us on their side, too. This is supremely important in the day in which we are living. Regardless of our political views, God is asking us to pray for the person He decides to put into office. We have not been faithful in this area. Father, please forgive us!

When we choose to pray for all people in this way – especially those who are in authority over us, our lives are peaceful and quiet, and we are filled with godliness and dignity. This is God's promised land.

PRAY FOR PEOPLE TO TURN TO JESUS

It is impossible to receive Jesus without turning toward Him. We are going the wrong way. So, if we want a person to know Jesus, we must ask God to turn their heart toward Him and have His Spirit draw them toward Himself.

"But whenever someone turns to the Lord, the veil is taken away. For the Lord is the Spirit, and wherever the Spirit of the Lord is, there is freedom. So all of us who have had that veil removed can see and reflect the glory of the Lord. And the Lord – who is the Spirit – makes us more and more like Him as we are changed into His glorious image." (2 Corinthians 3:16-18).

If anyone turns to the Lord, something magical happens. The veil is removed. The Lord sets us free, and we can see! We can really see Jesus. Then we can reflect His glory: love, joy, peace, patience, kindness, goodness, gentleness, faithfulness, self-control. Pray for people to turn!

PRAY FOR PEOPLE TO OPEN THEIR HEART WIDE

Most people have closed hearts. They are guarded toward people and toward God, but no one can receive anything from God unless they open their hearts to receive. So, we pray for hearts to open wide.

Jesus said, "Look! I stand at the door and knock. If you hear My voice and open the door, I will come in, and we will share a meal together as friends." (Revelation 3:20). A friend! Jesus is a friend who is always standing at the door knocking. Pray that they will open the door and let Him in.

We can also speak to the heart – we prophesy.

> "Open up, ancient gates!
> Open up, ancient doors,

and let the King of glory enter.
Who is the King of glory?
The LORD, strong and mighty;
the LORD, invincible in battle.
Open up, ancient gates!
Open up, ancient doors
and let the King of glory enter.
Who is the King of glory?
The LORD of Heaven's Armies –
He is the King of glory." (Psalm 24:7-10).

If that heart opens up, the LORD of Heaven's Armies will enter to fight their battles. He is strong and mighty and invincible. He will win. He is the King of glory!

PRAY FOR EYES TO SEE AND EARS TO HEAR AND A HEART TO UNDERSTAND

His disciples came and asked Him, "Why do you use parables when you talk to the people?"

He replied, "You are permitted to understand the secrets of the Kingdom of Heaven, but others are not. To those who LISTEN to My teaching, more understanding will be given, and they will have an abundance of knowledge. But for those who are not listening, even what little understanding they have will be taken away from them. That is why I use these parables."

> 'For they look, but they don't really see.
> They hear, but they don't really listen or understand.'

This fulfills the prophecy of Isaiah that says,

> 'When you hear what I say,
> you will not understand.
> When you see what I do,
> you will not comprehend.
> For the hearts of these people are hardened,
> and their ears cannot hear,
> and they have closed their eyes –

>   so their eyes cannot see,
>   and their ears cannot hear,
>   and their hearts cannot understand,
>   and they cannot turn to Me
>   and let Me heal them.'

Without eyes to see and ears to hear and a heart to understand, we cannot turn to the Lord so that He can heal us. We must pray for God to open eyes so that they can see and ears that they can hear and hearts that they can understand.

"O send out Your light and Your truth; let them guide them. Let them lead them to Your holy mountain, to the place where You live." (Psalm 43:3).

"The LORD took hold of me, and I was carried away by the Spirit of the LORD to a valley filled with bones. He led me around among the bones that covered the valley floor. They were scattered everywhere across the ground and were completely dried out. Then He asked me, 'Son of man, can these bones become living people again?'"

"O Sovereign LORD," I replied, "You alone know the answer to that."

Then He said to me, "Speak a prophetic message to these bones and say, "Dry bones, LISTEN to the word of the LORD! This is what the Sovereign LORD says: Look! I am going to put breath into you and make you live again! I will put flesh and muscle on you and cover you with skin. I will put breath into you, and you will come to life. Then you will know that I am the LORD!"

So I spoke this message, just as He told me. Suddenly as I spoke, there was a rattling noise all across the valley. The bones of each body came together and attached themselves as complete skeletons. Then as I watched, muscle and flesh formed over the bones. Then skin formed to cover their bodies, but they still had no breath in them.

The He said to me, "Speak a prophetic message to the winds, son of man. Speak a prophetic message and say, 'This is what the Sovereign LORD says: Come, O breath, from the four winds! Breathe into these dead bodies so they may live again.'"

"So I spoke the message as He commanded me, and breath came into their bodies. They all came to life and stood up on their feel – a great army."

Then He said to me, "Son of man, these bones represent the people of Israel. They are saying, 'We have become old, dry bones – all hope is gone. Our nation is finished.' Therefore, prophesy to them and say, 'This is what the Sovereign LORD says: O My people, I will open your graves of exile and cause you to rise again. Then I will bring you back to the land of Israel. When this happens, O My people, you will know that I am the LORD. I will put My Spirit in you, and you will live again and return home to your own land. Then you will know that I, the LORD, have spoken, and I have done what I said. Yes, the LORD has spoken!"

A NEW HEART AND A NEW SPIRIT

"Therefore, give the people of Israel this message from the Sovereign LORD: I am bringing you back, but not because you deserve it. I am doing it to protect My holy name, on which you brought shame while you were scattered among the nations. I will show you how holy My great name is – the name on which you brought shame among the nations. And when I reveal My holiness through you before their very eyes, says the Sovereign LORD, then the nations will know that I am the LORD. For I will gather you up from all the nations and bring you home again to your land."

"Then I will sprinkle clean water on you, and you will be clean. Your filth will be washed away, and you will no longer worship idols. And I will give you a new heart, and I will put a new spirit in you. I will take out your stony, stubborn heart and give you a tender, responsive heart. And I will put My Spirit in you so that you will follow My decrees and be careful to obey My regulations."

"And you will live in Israel, the land I gave your ancestors long ago. You will be My people, and I will be your God. I will cleanse you of your filthy behavior. I will give you good crops of grain, and I will send no more famines on the land. I will give you great harvests from your fruit trees and fields, and never again will the surrounding nations be able to scoff at your land for its famines. Then you will remember your past sins and despise yourselves for all the detestable things you did. But remember, says the Sovereign LORD, I am not doing this because you deserve it. O My people of Israel, you should be utterly ashamed of all you have done!"

"This is what the Sovereign LORD says: When I cleanse you from your sins, I will repopulate your cities, and the ruins will be rebuilt. The fields that use to lie empty and desolate in plain view of everyone will again be farmed. And when I bring you back, people will say, 'This former wasteland is now like the Garden of Eden! The abandoned and ruined cities now have strong walls and are filled with people! Then the surrounding nations that survive will know that I, the LORD, have rebuilt the ruins and replanted the wasteland. For I, the LORD, have spoken, and I will do what I say."

"This is what the Sovereign LORD says: I AM READY TO HEAR ISRAEL'S PRAYERS and to increase their numbers like a flock. They will be as numerous as the sacred flocks that fill Jerusalem's streets at the time of her festivals. The ruined cities will be crowded with people once more, and everyone will know that I am the LORD." (Ezekiel 36:22-38).

God said that He is ready to hear our prayers. He said that He will sprinkle clean water on us, and we will be clean. Our filth will be washed away, and we will no longer worship idols. He said He will take out our stony, stubborn heart and put in a tender, responsive heart. He said that our wastelands will be like the Garden of Eden – not because we deserve it, because we don't. This is such a precious promise from God who wants to reveal His holiness through His people, and He wants us to ask Him to do it. Read this several times. Pray it. Let's watch and see what God does.

PRAY FOR PEOPLE TO KNOW GOD

"I have not stopped thanking God for you. I pray for you constantly, asking God, the glorious Father of our Lord Jesus Christ, to give you spiritual wisdom and insight so that you might grow in your knowledge of God. I pray that your hearts will be flooded with light so that you can understand the confident hope He has given to those He called – His holy people who are His rich and glorious inheritance."

"I also pray that you will understand the incredible greatness of God's power for us who believe Him. This is the same mighty power that raised Christ from the dead and seated Him the place of honor at God's right hand in the heavenly realms. Now He is far above any ruler or authority or power or leader or anything else – not only in this world but also in the world to come. God has put all things under the authority of Christ and has made Him head over all things for the benefit of the church. And the church is His body; it is made full and complete by Christ, who fills all things everywhere with Himself." (Ephesians 1:16-23).

Wow. To know Him! For hearts to be flooded with light and understanding! To understand the greatness of His power! To know Jesus – the One who fills all things everywhere with Himself! May we all know Him!

WHEN TIMES GET HARD

We are living in hard times, and they are going to get harder, so we pray for one another.

"I fall to my knees and pray to the Father, the Creator of everything in heaven and on earth. I pray that from His glorious, unlimited resources He will empower you with inner strength through His Spirit. Then Christ will make His home in your hearts as you trust in Him. Your roots will grow down into God's love and it will keep you strong. And may you have the power to understand, as all God's people should, how wide, how long, how high, and how deep His love is. May you EXPERIENCE the love of Christ, though it is too great to understand fully. Then you will be made complete with all the fullness of life and power that comes from God." (Ephesians 3:14-19).

We are asking that the God of the Universe, the Creator of everything would strengthen and empower the people we are praying for with inner strength so that Christ will make His home in their hearts as the TRUST Him. What do they need? Patience? Endurance? Encouragement? Hope? Joy? From His glorious, unlimited resources, God has everything we need. Wow! That is a lot to unpack. We can ask God to give people everything they need to make it.

But then on top of that, we ask that they would be able to understand

and experience how high and wide and long and deep Christ's love is. To understand and experience the love of Christ – this love that is completely past understanding. Oh, my goodness! Then they will be made complete with all the fullness of life and power that comes from God. This prayer is big. I pray it often. I pray it loud. I pray it when I wake up and when I go to sleep. I pray it for everyone who is struggling.

PRAY FOR WISDOM

We all need wisdom. There is a Scripture in Isaiah 11 that I have been praying for years. I pray it for all people who are in leadership positions in the church, in the work place, in official positions of power. I pray it for my husband and my sons. I pray it for those I love. I pray it for myself. I want all people to have wisdom.

"Out of the stump of David's family will grow a shoot – yes, a new Branch bearing fruit from the old root. And the Spirit of the LORD will rest on him – the Spirit of wisdom and understanding, the Spirit of counsel and might, the Spirit of knowledge and the fear of the LORD. He will delight in obeying the LORD. He will not judge by appearance nor make a decision based on hearsay. He will give justice to the poor and make fair decisions for the exploited. The earth will shake at the force of his word, and one breath from his mouth will destroy the wicked. He will wear righteousness like a belt and truth like an undergarment."

"In that day the wolf and the lamb will live together; the leopard will lie down with the baby goat. The calf and the yearling will be safe with the lion, and a little child will lead them all. The cow will graze near the bear. The cub and the calf will lie down together. The lion will eat hay like a cow. The baby will play safely near the hole of a cobra. Yes, a little child will put its hand in a nest of deadly snakes without harm. Nothing will hurt or destroy in all My holy mountain, for as the waters fill the sea, so the earth will be filled with people who know the LORD." (Isaiah 11:1-9).

When the Spirit of wisdom in all of its forms falls on God's people, we will not judge by appearance or make decisions by hearsay. We will delight in obeying God. We will speak what is right, and it will shake the earth. We will wear righteousness like a belt and truth like an undergarment, and NOTHING will hurt or destroy in all of this holy mountain. I want the Spirit of wisdom to fall on all people so badly. Then all things will be made right.

I don't know if this chapter is stirring your heart, but it is surely stirring mine. It is time to pray. If we truly believed that God hears and answers every prayer we pray, we would be on our knees right now. "The end of the world is coming soon. Therefore, let us be earnest and disciplined in our prayers." (1 Peter 4:7).

16. CONCLUSION

We are living in crazy times. No one has to tell us. We know. Nothing makes sense. Lies and deception are everywhere. Division. Hatred. Greed. Lust. Pride. Chaos. Nothing is solid. And yet, we were all created for such a time as this. We were hand-picked by God, chosen to be the hands and feet of Jesus.

In this world that is covered in absolute darkness, God's love is going to shine brightly. Patience. Kindness. Goodness. Gentleness. Loyalty. Honor. LOVE. Unfailing love. Sacrificial love. Genuine love.

When I started writing this book in the spring of this year, I knew none of this. It came quickly. I embraced every word. Now I am attempting to live every word. It feels like my feet are on solid ground. It feels like my roots are going deep. It feels like springtime. Refreshing waters. Cool breezes. Gentle flowing rivers. Spring rains. Meadows. Flowers. Majestic Mountains. Quiet. Peaceful. Secure.

This is not a book you read; this is a book you live, a book to be embraced, a grace gift to God's people. It is my prayer that you will lay hold of the gift that is in front of you. May this, God's Word, be exalted and spread quickly. May God's Kingdom advance, and His holy name be honored. May these seeds fall on fertile soil, and may it produce a hundred-fold harvest of righteousness in your life and in the lives of those you love. May there be a stirring inside of you that is so high and wide and long and deep that you cannot get away from it. Deep calling to deep. May the longing to know God and to become like Him never let you go. May everyone who sees you, see Jesus, and may your light shine brightly throughout all eternity. I am asking this in the mighty, magnificent name of Jesus.

"Now all glory to God, who is able, through His mighty power at work within us, to accomplish infinitely more than we might ask or think. Glory to Him in the church and in Christ Jesus through all generations forever and ever!" (Ephesians 3:20-21). Amen.

OTHER RESOURCES

TRAINED IN RIGHTEOUSNESS:
Equipping the Saints for Such a Time as This
By Terri Tidwell

THE PROPHETS SPEAK
By Terri Tidwell

www.witnesshimnow.com

ABOUT THE AUTHOR

Terri Tidwell is a wife, a mother, and a grandmother. She is a lover of God and of all things good. Her greatest desire is to become less so that God can become more.

Made in the USA
Monee, IL
07 October 2024